DAMAGED GOODS

DAMAGED GOODS

New Perspectives on
CHRISTIAN PURITY

Dianna E. Anderson

JERICHO
BOOKS

New York   Boston   Nashville

Where names appear with first name and surname, that is the person's real name. Where names appear with only a first name, that is a pseudonym chosen to respect the privacy of the person who has shared their story with me.

Jericho Books
Hachette Book Group
1290 Avenue of the Americas
New York, NY 10104

JerichoBooks.com

Printed in the United States of America

RRD-C

First edition: February 2015
10 9 8 7 6 5 4 3 2 1

Jericho Books is an imprint of Hachette Book Group, Inc.
The Jericho Books name and logo are trademarks of Hachette Book Group, Inc.

The Hachette Speakers Bureau provides a wide range of authors for speaking events. To find out more, go to www.HachetteSpeakersBureau.com or call (866) 376-6591.

The publisher is not responsible for websites (or their content) that are not owned by the publisher.

Library of Congress Cataloging-in-Publication Data

Anderson, Dianna E.
  Damaged goods : new perspectives on Christian purity / Dianna E. Anderson. — First edition.
     pages cm
  Includes bibliographical references.
  ISBN 978-1-4555-7739-2 (hardcover) — ISBN 978-1-4555-7737-8 (ebook)
  1. Virginity—Religious aspects—Christianity.   2. Chastity.   3. Sex—Religious aspects—Christianity.   I. Title.
  BV4647.C5A554 2015
  241'.664—dc23
                              2014013843

For my mother,
the first feminist I ever knew.

Contents

I Was a Teenage Virgin

The lights are down low, and the dance floor is lit and waiting. Soft music is playing over the speakers. A row of young women, dressed in their finest, fanciest clothing, are waiting on one side for their dates to come ask them to dance. There's not much middle school fidgeting and nervousness about who's going to ask whom—each girl knows exactly whom she's going to dance with and she's known him her entire life. She's made pledges and vows to this person already in the evening, and is now ready to spend time dancing and celebrating with him.

Their dates—their fathers—and they are ready to celebrate the commitments each of them made tonight. Each father committed to being a good, godly, guiding force in his daughter's life. And each daughter committed to keeping herself pure and unsullied until the day her father gives her away to her husband. This is a purity ball.

According to statistics, of the hundred young girls gathered tonight, eighty will not make it to their wedding night as a virgin. Sadly, some of them have already been violated

1

sexually. Still more will be coerced into sexual encounters they don't want to have by a boyfriend, by an acquaintance at a party, by someone they trust. More will fall in love and say yes to someone who, for one reason or another, they will not marry. Many others will realize that they are not attracted to men or that they are unable to marry. Purity balls—a growing but still obscure phenomenon—started in Colorado in the mid-1990s. But the zeitgeist that made them popular had been building for decades, snowballing in intensity in the United States for years.

I was brought up in the evangelical purity movement. At fourteen years old, standing in front of my entire church with my parents, I pledged to save myself for marriage. I delved into reading the guides, learning about purity and how to keep myself pure, for years. I held myself and others to the high standards of purity that the church set for us.

One of the most disappointing moments of my young life came when I was brave enough to say to one of my best friends, "I think I like you as more than a friend."

We were at a small Christian college together. He had transferred there during my sophomore year. We'd met at a Christian summer camp a couple of years before. I'd liked him for years. I had a habit of falling in love with the guys who were my best friends, leading to nights of crying myself to sleep in my dorm room. Influenced by the archaic gender roles taught within the purity movement, I was determined that the man should make the first move— were I to say anything, it would upset the balance and ultimately doom the relationship. So I pined, sometimes not so quietly, hoping that the men I was falling for would somehow read my mind.

By the time I was a junior in college, I'd decided that

being honest was a better policy than sobbing into my pillow. Telling a boy I liked him was scary, but it would spare me the pain that came with the "friend zone." So one October Sunday, I decided enough was enough, and sent my friend Ethan an e-mail: "Let's go on a walk. I have something to talk to you about."

"Sure. Meet me after church."

I threw on my oversize college hoodie and ran a comb through my short hair. I was much more concerned with what I was about to say than with what I would look like while saying it. We met in the lobby of the dorm we both lived in—he on the first floor and I on the third. We headed down the sidewalk in silence. I was figuring out how to say things, and he was clearly waiting for me to speak.

"The thing is, Ethan"—I stumbled over my words—"I like you as more than a friend." I watched him carefully to see his reaction.

His shoulders slumped and he sighed. "That's what I thought you were going to say."

Here it was: my rejection. In my gut, I knew this would happen, but I wasn't prepared for why. Ethan had had a girlfriend previously and they'd broken up a few months before. He explained, "I sort of thought this was coming. But I don't think you want to be in a relationship with me. I have too much baggage."

"Baggage? What baggage? What are you talking about? I can handle anything."

We were stopped at a light, waiting for a walk signal to cross.

He looked straight at me. "I'm not a virgin, Dianna. My ex and I had sex, and that's not what you want."

I was speechless. And not because he assumed I wasn't

3

prepared for a relationship with a guy who was experienced. But because he was right—I wasn't. I instantly reshuffled his position in my life from "potential suitor" to "damaged goods—not marriage material ever." The look on my face gave my thoughts away, and he turned back toward campus, explaining, "I can tell by the look on your face that you're not ready for any of this. I need to deal with this sort of thing myself. I don't think I'm prepared to get into a relationship with someone who doesn't know these experiences and that's really all I can say about it."

My thoughts ran rampant: Did I even know him? Why couldn't he have waited? What other sins were people hiding from me?

Our environment, permeated by purity culture, commanded that he be ashamed, a pariah, and that I judge him. Ethan was just one in a long string of friends I would judge for their sexual choices. And I felt justified in judging them because my theology and culture justified it. I had to shame my friends for their choices, I thought: it was the only way they would learn.

That conversation is one of many I regret. I lost a friend that day, though it took a few years for the relationship to fully fall apart. I have regretted nothing more in my life than that I wasn't a true friend to those who were suffering under the weight of such shame, a friend who could help them understand that God does not function in a culture of shame.

A few years later, I found myself on the receiving end of the same type of judgment when I began to opine that perhaps the Bible wasn't as clear as we think it is on the issue of premarital sex. I'd not even done anything sexually "sinful" at that point, but as I began to study the issues more, I received a flurry of messages from family members that I was choosing feminism over Christianity and justifying sinful living. One message said I was questioning the Scripture about sex because I couldn't get Christian men to sleep with me, so I was moving toward feminism to find people who would. Ouch.

I realized how wrong I'd been to judge Ethan. I examined my sanctimonious declarations about virginity. I faced the culture I'd been hiding behind, one that heaped shame on others. Purity culture says what matters most about a person is whether or not they have had sex in the "wrong" ways. It makes wearing a white dress at her wedding the marker of morality for a woman.

I began to pray about how to atone for my sins of shame and gracelessness. Over the course of preparing to write this book, I spoke to Christians aged twenty to fifty, from various faith backgrounds, all over the United States—missionary kids, women of color, suburban whites, women who like women, and men who like men. Across the spectrum, they reflected on a culture of judgment, pain, and shame. They had experienced these things because of choices they had made and options that had been taken from them. I listened to story after story of being unable to feel close to God because of shame, being kicked out of one's home, losing friends, separation from one's faith community. No atonement was good enough, no sacrifice or apology could erase the shame these people bore. They were forever marked with the scarlet brand of "slut" because they had not waited until their wedding day.

A generation of Christian women and men, girls and boys, is broken and hurting from the sexual dysfunction and shame of purity culture. Many grew up being told over and over that their virginity was the most important thing they could give their spouse on their wedding night, only to reach that point and realize that having saved themselves didn't magically create sexual compatibility or solve their marital issues. Many soon divorced. Still others sat silently in their church groups, wondering what virginity could possibly mean for them as people who had been victims of incest or abuse or who felt attracted to the same gender.

We've been told a lie that our worth lies in what we do (or don't do) with our genitals. According to the proponents of Christian purity, we are "damaged goods." We are afraid to own our physicality. We do not know our own bodies and, therefore, we do not truly know ourselves. We are afraid to express ourselves sexually. We do not have language to talk about the nuances of existing as a sexual being.

This book aims to develop a Christian ethic that doesn't center around saying no, but through which we learn how to say a "godly yes." We are not broken and we are not alone. As God's creatures, we are created to be expressive, to love and live without shame. God does not function in a currency of shame and stigma. God does not cast us out of community; God loves us through community. God's children are never "damaged goods."

The roots of shame run deep, and it takes patience, challenge, anger, and grace to pull them all out. My hope is that you will find help on these pages to break free from shame and to avoid passing the sometimes well-intentioned lies of purity culture to coming generations.

I love the Church, and I believe firmly that in teaching purity doctrines and promoting purity culture we have lost our way. We have forgotten justice and mercy in the name of legalism. We have deviated from a God of grace and love and mercy and instead embraced a cold, distant, heartless God who does not care about individual contexts and individual experiences. We in the American church have allowed political interests and sinful systems to dictate our theology. We must examine ourselves and the pain we cause, then take responsibility for the shame we heap on believers and say to ourselves, "No more."

Youth are leaving the church in droves, many because they feel they cannot live up to its demands about purity. It is time to create a new way of thinking, a new way to love our neighbors as Jesus commanded. That means Christian life that expresses a healthy sexuality of mutual pleasure and mutual consent.

Poet Gerard Manley Hopkins wrote the following in "God's Grandeur":

The world is charged with the grandeur of God.
It will flame out, like shining from shook foil...

As God's people, we have tried to quell the flames, tried to make God's grandeur fit into our predetermined boxes and theories and theologies. It is time to listen for the Spirit that hovers over the world and, as Hopkins says, "broods with warm breast and with ah! bright wings." God is in the pain, the hurt, and the shame. God is with the ones, like Ethan, whom I once called damaged goods. This is a chance to listen to the Spirit of Truth about what sexual purity really is.

CHAPTER TWO

A Review of the Christian Purity Movement

To understand how the purity movement in evangelical culture has been changing the landscape of American churches, we must roll back the clock to a century before now. Sociologist Kristin Luker and several others in her field propose that it was at the beginning of the twentieth century, not during the 1960s, that the real sexual revolution began to take place. Indeed, it was amid the bobbed hair, short skirts, and heavy drinking of the 1920s that public health and sexual education programs began. Of course, back then they weren't called sexual education, but rather "social hygiene" programs. Begun out of a sense of fear and xenophobia, these new programs sought to restore the balance to America's systems of class and race.

According to Luker, the meaning of sexual activity within society was shifting. The growing influence of industrialization had wrecked the previous stratification between the classes. Urbanization of much of the population had created a new class of young men and women who worked and partied together. And the labor rights movement and a shift in the scientific view of what being an "adult" meant—age and maturity rather than economic independence—created a new class of young people termed *adolescents*. These adolescents challenged numerous social norms: the women cut off their hair, wore shorter skirts, drank and partied and had sex.

Many of the trends that worry conservatives in my generation also worried the older members of the white, educated upper classes in the early twentieth century. Divorce was on the rise. Marriage was being delayed because young people were working more. Women were "acting like men" in the bedroom. And marriage was losing its institutional hold in society.

Venereal diseases were spreading throughout not only the lower classes but the upper echelons of society as well. Syphilis was a large threat—that generation's equivalent of HIV/AIDS in the eighties—and the widespread presence of prostitution in urban centers helped the disease spread. Sexual education, reformers thought, would stem the tide of prostitution—at least the men thought—by instilling moral standards among the nation's young men. Many of the women in these groups felt that prostitution exemplified a sexual double standard for men and women—that being a "whore" was a threat to a woman's reputation and something she could never recover from, while the men who frequented her were given a pass.

Social hygiene groups consisting of educated elites and religious figures proposed that an education on the proper understanding of sex—as an act of intimacy within marriage to bring people together—would be an adequate response to these new trends and problems. But this view of sex as

intimate was itself a new one in American society. Throughout the nineteenth century, sex had been closely tied to
procreation, but with the advent of newer birth control
technologies (technologies, it's worth noting, that weren't
accessible to the lower classes), sex as an expression of intimacy was becoming the word of the day. Luker writes:

> In the face of this shift, the social hygienists turned
> to education—teaching people not so much about
> sex as about marriage. They took for granted that
> their task was to educate Americans about "whole-
> some" sex, which for them meant wholesome sex
> within marriage. In fact, what they were really up
> to was recruiting sex to support a new model of
> marriage-as-intimacy, then emerging among the
> middle and upper classes.[1]

It's remarkable how similar the struggle of social hygiene
groups in the 1920s was to conservative Christians' push
against comprehensive sexual education today. The theme
is almost identical: modern culture is devaluing sex and
marriage and intimacy, and we must find a way to bring
their value back. Social hygienists of a century ago sought
to remedy this problem by educating Americans about intimacy, by trumpeting the enjoyment of sex within marriage,
and by educating people about their bodies. Conservative
Christians of the modern day pursue much the same goals,
but they do so in reverse. Many believe that explicit knowledge about bodies and their functions will encourage sexual
activity, so they promote abstinence-only, marriage-centered
education. They believe that centering the procreative pur-
poses of sex within the conversation is important to respond

to the "homosexuality problem"—a reversal of the position of their forerunners, who promoted sex as an expression of intimacy.

The reason for this reversal in tactics arrived in the middle of the century.

Baby Boomers and the Free-Love Sixties

Let's fast-forward a few years to World War II. Feminist ire was already building prior to the war, with women being granted the vote and the "loose morals" of the 1920s changing and shaping the ways in which men and women related to each other. During the war, as men were shipped off overseas to fight, rationing and poverty at home created a need within communities to support the war effort. Women (white middle-class women in particular) stepped up. They took over jobs previously reserved for men—hard factory jobs, manufacturing the weapons of war. They wore pants and got grease in their hair and calluses on their hands and participated in generally unladylike behavior. They tasted blood and knew they were capable.

Following the war, many men returned home. The baby boom happened and the United States set about fighting communist influence around the world. Having ceded parts of Germany to the USSR, and engaged in a war in Korea fighting Russian communist influence on the peninsula, America placed utmost importance on patriotism. According to Stephanie Coontz, author of the 1992 seminal work on the American family *The Way We Never Were*, this social change following WWII was a new phenomenon. For the first time in nearly a hundred years, among white people, the age of first marriage dropped for both genders and the divorce rate also decreased. Fertility went up and the nuclear family formed. But, according to Coontz, this kind of "traditional" family was a new invention—rather than being a microcosm of what America symbolized, the 1950s nuclear family was a new and foreign concept. The "traditional family," in other words, is an invention of my parents' generation.[2]

In this period, doing your part meant being a white middle-class family with a picket fence and a house in the suburbs. But white suburban women—women who knew the value of a hard day's work and had bled for the war effort alongside their men—were disillusioned. Feminist writer Betty Friedan published *The Feminine Mystique* and challenged the role of women as "perfect housewives" in the fight against communism. And with that, the second wave of feminism began.

This feminism was bolder and more salacious than the feminism that had come before it—instead of fighting for the right to vote, the feminists of the 1960s were fighting for the right to have control of their own bodies, to love whom they wanted to love, and to leave abusive husbands and find their own careers in the work force. Concurrent with this feminist revolution—which involved mainly white women fighting for white-oriented goals—the Civil Rights movement of the South was changing the political climate.

By the 1970s the United States was in turmoil. We were embroiled in yet another conflict against communism— this time in Vietnam—and the draft had conscripted many young men again. An increasing police state at home—as exemplified by the shooting at Kent State, where police

opened fire on an antiwar protest, killing four students—
was resulting in distrust in the government. This distrust
was solidified further when President Nixon resigned amid
allegations that he was involved in criminal activity.

Over what sociologists remark is a very short time—a
period of just five or so years—the aftershocks of the first
sexual revolution radiated through the American population and radically changed the way we look at sex. In
1965, an unwed pregnant woman would either be shuffled
off into a shotgun wedding or hidden from view with a
relative in another town—such was the shame of such an
obvious indication that she had had sex outside of marriage.
According to Luker, public opinion polls back up this view
of the time: 70 percent of Americans believed premarital
sex outside of marriage was morally wrong.

But between 1965 and 1975, social views radically
shifted, and government policy quickly shifted with them.
The legalization of hormonal birth control in 1965 and
the legalization of abortion in 1973 moved sexual activity
out of the public sphere and into the private. With sex no
longer a public health concern, people were free to make
sexual decisions without the threat of public scorn. Women
were more in control of their reproduction than ever before,
which allowed many of them to leave abusive marriages,
to delay marriage, and to begin, as the common narrative
would put it, "acting like men"—both in the office and in
the bedroom.

For evangelical Christians, this time was just as tumul-
tuous. A stark racial divide in the American church meant
that many white conservative Christians found themselves
on the wrong side of the Civil Rights movement. They
were seeing their young women swayed by a feminism that

openly and actively argued against the idea of gendered roles for women, something much of the church took for granted. Pregnancies outside of wedlock (for white girls) were beginning to be viewed less as something shameful and more as something that required social support. Suddenly America the Christian Nation was proving itself not so Christian anymore. Luker writes:

> Implicit in the sexual revolution, and especially in the changing standards of female behavior, was the threatening idea that people—particularly women, the traditional guardians of the home—were having sex for their own reasons. Sex was no longer part of a courtship process that would lead to a spiritualized eroticism designed to confine more entertaining, more satisfying sex neatly to the marital bedroom. Now sex was just another pleasure, to be indulged in whenever two parties agreed. Worse yet, although sex educators largely recognized this only in the context of teenage pregnancy, people who were having sex just for fun were increasingly moving on to the next stage, building families without bothering to get married.[3]

The Moral Majority and the Purity Push

The period following the sexual revolution witnessed the rise of the Moral Majority and the religious right. In the 1970s evangelicals were scared of what they saw happening on the national scene. Free-love, antiwar, and, as they perceived it, anti-American sentiments were challenging the traditional and patriarchal world in which they had thrived for so many years. Previously preachers like Jerry Falwell had believed strongly in the separation of religion and politics, and even preached sermons to this effect—in 1964's "Ministers and Marches" sermon, he proclaimed that "preachers are not called to be politicians, but soul winners."[4]

But the advent of widely available contraception and the 1973 Roe v. Wade ruling changed all that. The growing liberalization of society, as Christians saw it, threatened the all-American family structure. Falwell and many other evangelicals realized they had to do something in response to this tectonic social shift.

In 1976 the evangelical right began its own sexual revolution—a return to what it viewed as the roots of Biblical values. According to Janice M. Irvine, author of *Talk About Sex*, a history of sexual education and evangelicalism in America, evangelicals in the 1970s responded to the changes that had taken place since the sixties by creating their own alternative sexuality industry. Tim and Beverly LaHaye published a watershed book—*The Act of Marriage: The Beauty of Sexual Love*, and launched a movement focused on purity and abstinence. Evangelicals were getting in on the sexual revolution in their own way.

As Irvine puts it:

Evangelicals began to celebrate sex, but only divinely approved sex. Evangelicals believe that there are absolute truths for sexual morality, known throughout the Bible. Despite their own growing participation in a public sexual arena, they are critics of a "sex saturated culture where not much is really sacred." For example, strictures against masturbation had markedly relaxed since the end of the nineteenth century, in part through the efforts of modern sexologists....[But] the LaHayes warned in 1976 that "we do not feel it is an acceptable practice for Christians."[5]

Riding the coattails of the rising evangelical movement, in 1979 Falwell founded a political entity called the Moral Majority. This conservative Christian lobbying group capitalized on evangelical fear of change, and lobbied for conservative policy at all levels of government. It reversed the previous fundamentalist position of disinterest in politics and instead began to center the political conversation within Christianity. While the group itself dissolved in the 1980s—having lasted only a few short years on the political scene—the mark it left on evangelicalism in America affected an entire generation of women born into this reactionary post-1970s time period.

Falwell's theology capitalized on and modernized aspects of Christian sexual ethics that had been taken for granted. Previously people outside the church had shamed young women who got themselves "in trouble," resulting in societal reinforcement of supposed Christian ethics. Secular society and the church were mostly synchronistic in terms of "family values." "Purity" was not being challenged, and therefore did not need to be defended. But values shifted rapidly following the sexual revolution of the sixties. As Luker tells us (emphasis original):

Thus the watershed of the sexual revolution and all it stood for [was when] women, whose ties to motherhood were loosened, started to become *individuals*...

who claimed they were different in no essential way from men. Public opinion agreed; not only did American attitudes and behavior regarding both sex and gender change, and change rapidly, these changes diffused quickly among different sectors of society.[6]

These rapid changes, over the course of a decade, resulted in whiplash for the American church. Now the evangelical church—in itself a fairly new movement—found itself having to define and emphasize its boundaries around sexual activity and what marriage and family looked like. In response to a combination of demographic decline, increased use of contraception, and an increasingly outspoken gay rights movement, evangelical America returned to the view of sex as procreative. This view contradicted that of the forerunners of the moral sexual reform movement, who had sought to reignite interest in sex within marriage by emphasizing the pleasure and intimacy of the act. Instead, to right demographic shifts and to bring America back around to being a "Christian nation," evangelicals in America began to rally against what they called a "genocide of the unborn," arguing against both contraception and abortion. And they did so primarily by focusing on the purity of their daughters.

Youth Groups and the Rise of the Adolescent

Interestingly, shifts in church structure aided the intensity of the purity movement. Prior to the recognition of "adolescent" as a stage of development in the early twentieth century, church bodies rarely separated ministries by age past the age of twelve, though they did separate by gender on occasion. But in the 1940s, that all began to change. A young preacher named Jim Rayburn began a new ministry aimed at teenagers called Young Life—a ministry that still exists today.[7] The popular ministry coincided with a Youth for Christ movement that turned into teen-focused Bible studies in the fifties and sixties. Adolescents were now seen as a viable demographic to focus on in the church, and their already-thriving presence across the nation became a fertile ground for politically minded purity ministries.

Indeed, Falwell's legacy is not the political weight of the Moral Majority, which disbanded in 1989 largely thanks to its massive unpopularity. Rather, Falwell's legacy is a focus on reaching young people, which he did through his conservatively minded Christian college, Liberty University. The emphasis on young people not only as important for the health of the church but also as important politically, should their power be harnessed, was not missed by the evangelical crowd of the 1970s.

The rise of youth ministries created the perfect guinea pig audience for the new and improved purity movement. As part of a culture focused on entertainment and social issues, youth groups became havens for culture war discussions, places where discipleship involved engagement with political issues from a conservative perspective—particularly those issues having to do with sex. In an effort to respond to the teen pregnancy crisis of the 1970s, youth-focused purity movement theology sought to return sex to its supposedly rightful place as a public issue, and to position the Christian family at the center. Numerous evangelical organizations sprang up to politicize the pushback against the sexual revolution and educate those involved—including Dr. James Dobson's radio-show-turned-evangelical-Goliath, Focus on the Family.[8]

Purity Movements and Abstinence-Only Education in the 1990s

In the 1990s, comprehensive sexual education was becoming more prevalent in public school systems, and churches began to use their youth ministries to provide different, countercultural messaging. By the end of the 1990s, purity had become an industry. The first purity ball was hosted in Colorado Springs, Colorado—home of Dobson's Focus on the Family ministry—by a small family who wanted to emphasize a father's role in guiding his daughters. The trend spread across the evangelical Midwest, eventually arriving in my hometown of Sioux Falls, South Dakota, and finding footholds in small religious communities.

Evangelical Christians from this era—beginning in 1990 and continuing to the present day—have been exposed to a continued emphasis on chastity, godly purity, and virginity. Many of my peers took a pledge to remain pure until their wedding day, and many who broke that vow suffered from intense shame and guilt over it. Sexual purity has become the one means by which the evangelical church separates itself from "the world." Endeavoring to claim the title of *counterculture*, the modern evangelical church responds to what it sees as a sexually permissive culture by locking down on purity and virginity and creating strict, harsh rules around what men and women can do with their bodies.

While abstinence-only education funding existed prior to the 1990s thanks to a 1981 law called the Adolescent Family Life Act (AFLA), such funding was challenged by various clergy and the American Civil Liberties Union and deemed unconstitutional in 1985. This decision was reversed by the US Supreme Court in 1988.[9] Funding through Title XX (federal monies for social services programs) stalled until President Clinton's massive welfare reform programs in the mid-1990s. Concerns about declining marriage rates and fear about teenage sexual activity meant that one of the largest of these programs funded abstinence-only (teaching abstinence as the only effective sexual health method) and abstinence-plus (giving some information about contraceptive use) education.

By 2003, abstinence-only education was the norm in public schools across the nation. While federal funding monies are not supposed to be used for religious or faith-based organizational lessons, the sheer vastness of the programs and the lack of oversight creates an environment where schools will use faith-based resources until they get caught. The prevalence of abstinence-only education is one of the most lasting effects of the reactionary evangelical politics of the 1980s.

As a result, the purity movement is not experienced only by women in the church but is working to exact social change among even those who do not share Christian religious convictions.

The development of purity as both a philosophy and a movement is a new phenomenon. Notably, the purity movement is responding to the very same concerns that puzzled social hygienists a century ago. These concerns about marriage and family aren't unique to my generation, but the concerned church must adapt to new social structures and ideas if it hopes to continue to make a difference. Healthy practices of marriage and family must be developed around new principles that honor the work and lives of individual people.

Loving One's Neighbor: How Purity Strayed from Its Purpose

Sexual purity—rather than a relationship with Jesus, caring for the poor, or loving one's neighbor—has become the marker of a good Christian in purity culture. While noble in intent, the purity movement has resulted in a destructive path of harmful misogyny and exclusion. Sexuality is not the center of a person's life, faith, or health. Yet an unbalanced and improper understanding of sexuality can put everything else in life off-kilter.

The purity movement, no matter how well intentioned, has, like many reactionary movements, become so harsh, fundamentalist, and rules-oriented that the idealistic goals it began with have been lost. The Christian right responded to changing times by instituting legalistic rules rather than grace, forgiveness, and mercy. Failure to follow the rules meant you had failed God and your church community. The evangelical purity movement lost the plot. The women of my generation (and sometimes the men, as in the case of Ethan) have borne the brunt of the destructive aftermath of our parents' reactionary doctrine.

The evangelical purity movement must be replaced with shame-free sexual ethics and a healthy understanding of ourselves as creations of God.

CHAPTER THREE

Let's Get Biblical: Sex in Scripture

Above my mom's desk in her home office is a decoration, carefully selected and placed among pictures of her children and the framed paintings of Rome I gave her as a present many years ago. I don't know when she acquired this piece, but it looks like something from Hobby Lobby or a Michaels craft store—one of those pieces made to look like you suddenly developed amazing handwriting and painted the words on the wood yourself. In front of a watermark of a bejeweled crown, the words read: "Whatever is Noble, Right, Pure, Lovely…Think On These Things."

The verse is Philippians 4:8, and is one I remember hearing time and again throughout my youth group years—with a special emphasis, naturally, on the word *pure*. We listened to speakers from national abstinence organizations, spent our time in small groups talking about how to be pure, and developed accountability to keep each other from lustful thoughts. We spent so much time talking about sex that I'm fairly surprised no one turned up pregnant out of sheer curiosity.

By the time I graduated from college, I had read all the books, had gone to all the events, and knew all the language to talk about how to keep pure. I absolutely *knew* that the Bible was clear that you shouldn't have sex until you're married—you shouldn't even have solo sex, which is Christianese for masturbation. The Bible was totally fundamentally clear on this fact. I'd believed so my entire life.

I believed—until I actually examined the ideas for myself. Purity proponents tend to repeat the same ideas over and over, and use the same proof texts over and over. They believe that sex is the binding act of marriage; that marriage is God-created and between one man and one woman for all time; that purity means no sexual thoughts or lust; that men and women *belong*—physically, metaphysically, emotionally, spiritually—to their spouses; and that the Bible clearly says that premarital sex is a sin.

We must deconstruct these myths about sex and the Bible.

Myth 1: Sex Makes People One Flesh

This particular idea is so pernicious that it is often simply accepted as fact. Pulling verses from both the Old and New Testaments, proponents of the purity movement argue that the story God tells about sex is one of a binding act, that from beginning to end in God's story, sex is what makes a marriage a marriage. Having sex with someone creates a lifelong marriage-like bond, which is why premarital sex is such a huge problem.

Married couple Eric and Leslie Ludy write in *When God Writes Your Love Story*:

God has set up a clear pattern for beautiful romance. We cannot experience the kind of love, sex, and intimacy we long for unless we follow His pattern. And His pattern is purity. Following His pattern means living in absolute faithfulness—body, mind and heart—to one person for a lifetime. It means honoring God's marriage covenant as sacred, saving every expression of sexual intimacy for *after* the covenant wedding vows are spoken. It means treating sexuality not as an opportunity to gratify selfish desires, but as an opportunity to selflessly serve our spouse.[10]

Joshua Harris, in *I Kissed Dating Goodbye*, writes:

Physical intimacy is much more than two bodies colliding. God designed our sexuality as a physical expression of the oneness of marriage. God guards it carefully and places many stipulations on it because He considers it extremely precious. A man and woman who commit their lives to each other gain the *right* to express themselves sexually to each other. A husband and wife may enjoy each other's bodies because they in essence belong to each other. But if you're not married to someone, you have no claim on that person's body, no right to sexual intimacy.[11]

In *Sex God*, Rob Bell comments that couples who are living together before marriage are "already [married] in

God's eyes, and maybe their having sex has already joined them as man and wife from God's perspective."[12]

From God's perspective, purity proponents say, having sex means that you're married, that you've made a commitment, and even if you've not made the vows, you're married in God's eyes. You have become one flesh.

Except...it's a lot more complicated than that. Bell draws his one-flesh interpretation from Exodus 22 and Deuteronomy 22—Old Testament laws about marriage. Harris and the Ludys frequently use Jesus's words on divorce, saying that the strict lines Jesus drew around divorce evince seriousness about the one-flesh-ness of sex. But these interpretations of both Old and New lack necessary context that complicates what God is supposedly saying about sex.

Deuteronomy, as part of the original Jewish Torah, is a dry book laying forth laws for the governance of Jewish society. It contains everything from warnings about proper hygiene in military encampments (Deuteronomy 23) to prohibitions against child sacrifice (Deuteronomy 18). And tucked in between laws about who can attend the religious assembly and what to do when you find an empty bird's nest, Deuteronomy 22:13–30 gives rules about sexual relations surrounding marriage. The rules (adapted from the New Revised Standard Version) are as follows:

1. If a man marries a woman, decides he doesn't like her, and tries to dissolve the marriage by claiming she wasn't a virgin at the time of the marriage, the father and mother of the bride must submit evidence of her virginity to the elders of the city. The father must show the elders

the bloody cloth from the wedding night as proof. If the groom is proven to be lying, he is fined a hundred shekels, and she stays his wife.

2. If, however, the charge of promiscuity is found to be true (if there is no evidence of virginity loss via bloody sheet), the bride will be stoned to death.

3. If a man is caught having an affair with another man's wife, he and the woman are to be stoned.

4. If a woman—a virgin, engaged to be married—is found in coitus with a man inside the city gates, they are both to be stoned, because she did not cry out (as she would in a situation of rape).

5. But if the woman is raped in the country, only her rapist will be stoned, because she did not commit an offense punishable by death, as she may have cried for help and not been heard.

6. But all this changes if the virgin woman is not engaged to be married—if she is raped, then the rapist simply owes her father fifty shekels of silver, and she will become his wife, and he is not permitted to divorce her.

7. And last, "a man shall not marry his father's wife."

In Biblical times a woman was the property of her husband, unable to own property on her own or have an identity apart from that of the man she was married to. Her "job" was to produce heirs to continue the family business and keep the genetic line going. Proof of virginity was therefore important to mark one's sons as property of the family. The proprietary, transactional nature of the marital relationship can be seen carried throughout the Deuteronomy passages, particularly with its commands on rape—rape is viewed as a theft of property, not a violation of a person.

This transactional nature of marriage is further reinforced in the next few verses about who is allowed to attend assembly—illegitimate sons and those unable to have natural heirs are excluded from the life of the Jewish assembly. The dehumanization of the wife in Old Testament marriage contracts is hardly a solid example of a one-flesh commandment.

With this as our Biblical basis, it's hard to view a one-flesh attitude toward sex as *honoring* to anyone—women didn't seem to get much of a say in whether they wanted to be bonded to these men, often in polygamous arrangements, for all time. And yet proponents of a one-flesh standard for purity point to these rules of transaction as proof.

However, others recognize the problematic nature of the Old Testament property laws, and point to Jesus's words on divorce throughout Matthew. In Matthew 19, Jesus is approached by the Pharisees and is asked about divorce point-blank:

> Some Pharisees came to him to test him. They asked, "Is it lawful for a man to divorce his wife for any and every reason?"
> "Haven't you read," he replied, "that at the beginning the Creator 'made them male and female,' and

said, 'For this reason a man will leave his father and mother and be united to his wife, and the two will become one flesh'? So they are no longer two, but one flesh. Therefore what God has joined together, let no one separate."

"Why then," they asked, "did Moses command that a man give his wife a certificate of divorce and send her away?"

Jesus replied, "Moses permitted you to divorce your wives because your hearts were hard. But it was not this way from the beginning. I tell you that anyone who divorces his wife, except for sexual immorality, and marries another woman commits adultery."[13]

Jesus here is saying that marriage is something that needs to be taken very, very seriously, because of the ways in which it changed the social standing and economic status of the people involved by removing them from their parents' house. The woman, at that time, was to stay in her father's house until she married, at which point she would move into a room on the side of her husband's father's house. This relationship forever changed the status of the woman. Jesus here does not speak against premarital sex or toward purity, but rather condemns the levity with which men of the age were approaching divorce.

In particular, the line about one flesh is not about sex, but rather about the ways in which marriage changed a person's status in society. Note that Jesus doesn't say, "The two are one flesh, therefore they are married." He positions the one-flesh statement—a hearkening back to the story of how Eve was created from a part of Adam—as following marriage. Marriage creates one flesh, rather than one flesh creating marriage. Marriage recreates, in a way, that unity of the Genesis story, after the two parts were first separated: when two people are brought together under the banner of love, it is good. It is a reminder of a Creator God and an eternal commitment, and therefore should not be taken lightly—sex or no sex.

During Jesus's time, a man could divorce his wife for any reason whatsoever—he found a prettier woman, she didn't prepare his dinner right, he didn't like her scarf that day, whatever suited his fancy. And the Jewish authorities were quite generous with divorce certificates, allowing men to leave their wives stranded. It is an understatement to say that divorce was a big deal during this time—divorce, for a woman, essentially meant destitution. Unable to own property, and unable to remarry because of the law, she would find herself impoverished and abandoned if she was divorced. Malachi 2:16 (NIV), for example, says, "'The man who hates and divorces his wife,' says the LORD, the God of Israel, 'does violence to the one he should protect.'"

Jesus's words both here and in the Sermon on the Mount evince an understanding of the carelessness with which men were leaving their wives destitute and alone—and indicts them for this sin. This sin, it is important to note, is not sexual in nature, but rather a sin of callousness and oppression. Rather than referring to sex as creating a marriage bond, the story God seems to be telling is one we find over and over in the Gospel—that the Christian is responsible to care for the hurting and the downtrodden, and should not be in the business of creating further pain.

Myth 2: One Man, One Woman
(and a Boatload of Concubines)

There aren't a lot of purity writers who address the marriages of the Old Testament, probably with good reason. We find a lot more of the idea of marriage as a heterosexual union between one man and one woman in the underlying assumptions about purity. Gender essentialism and exclusivity in marriage permeates nearly every work about Christian purity. *Dateable*, by Justin Lookadoo and Hayley DiMarco, is divided into sections "for Guys" and "for Girls." John and Stasi Eldredge wrote two separate books about the roles men and women play in coming together for marriage. Joshua Harris talks throughout *Sex Is Not the Problem (Lust Is)* about the differences between men and women and their approaches to marriage.

The assumption is clear: marriage is one man and one woman, forever.

Except when it isn't.

The unchecked and unpunished proliferation of polygamous marriages throughout the Old Testament undermines the idea that marriage is one man and one woman for all eternity. These marriages are hardly based on romance. Indeed, so rare in the Old Testament marriage is a romantic profession that we get only a few stories centered on the idea of marriage as love—most notably the story of Rachel, Leah, and Jacob.

Initially Jacob wanted to marry Rachel—he saw her and fell in love and wanted to have her for his wife. But her father set a price of indentured servitude for seven years. Jacob worked faithfully, and then, when it came time to marry, he was tricked into marrying Rachel's older sister Leah instead. But instead of giving up, Jacob was faithful to Leah and worked another seven years to earn Rachel's hand. But here's the catch: Jacob didn't divorce Leah and develop a monogamous relationship with Rachel. He was married to both women, he had children by both of them, and they lived together, albeit not all that happily, as there was much animosity between the sisters.

It's important here to realize that Jacob's initial marriage to Leah was of a transactional nature, and her children were still considered blessed by God for having been born of Jacob. Rachel's children, likewise, were blessed. There's no evidence—besides the animosity between the sisters—that such a polygamous arrangement was condemned or seen as unholy by God. Indeed, when this story is told in evangelical churches, Jacob is often held up as a positive example for staying faithful in his quest to marry Rachel and faithful in his marriage to Leah despite having been tricked. Purity doesn't seem to come into play in this story, except in that Rachel was kept waiting for fourteen years longer than she should have been.

Polygamy, in the vein of Rachel and Leah, was simply *the way things were* throughout the Old Testament. The variations on what marriage is and the ways in which marriage has evolved undermine the idea that purity evangelists are "simply obeying God," as they like to say. The fact that Solomon had concubines, that Abraham impregnated Hagar, that none of these acts were condemned (and some celebrated) should at least make us question the assumption that marriage exists only for one man and one woman.

Myth 3: Your Thoughts Are Sending You to Hell

Impurity starts long before the moments of passion in backseats. Instead it begins in our hearts, in our motivations and attitudes. "I tell you that anyone who looks on a woman lustfully has already committed adultery with her in his heart," Jesus plainly states....Sin begins in our minds and hearts.[14]

Joshua Harris, in the above quote, perfectly encapsulates the arguments against lust that are common throughout the purity movement. If we want a clean life, we must have a clean soul and mind. In Yoda-esque reasoning: thoughts lead to actions, actions to sex, sex to hell.

Striving for holiness is a worthy goal for the Christian, but in the eyes of the purity movement, you can never be too holy when it comes to your thoughts. Harris's second book, *Sex Is Not the Problem (Lust Is)*, offers advice on how to avoid potential lustfulness—including a recommendation to be disciplined about how you spend time in the bathroom (too long and your thoughts might wander and you'll discover yourself lusting, or worse, masturbating).

The verse Harris quotes above has been used to preach against any and all sexual arousal or thoughts—resulting in the suppression of natural sexual desires. It's important, then, when examining this particular verse, that we pay attention to the context that determines what *lust* means and what Jesus meant in the midst of the Sermon on the Mount. This verse—starting with "But"—does not occur in a vacuum. Indeed, it is surrounded by extreme hyperbole.

The verse immediately after commands men to gouge out their eyes if their eyes cause them to sin, and cut off their hands for the same offense. As a result, we must take the words of verse 28 with a grain of salt—Jesus is exaggerating here to make a larger point.

That point? That sin is not merely a matter of action, but of mental preparation for an act of sin. It is a repeated theme throughout the Bible that God looks at the heart, not just the actions of a person, and prizes a righteous heart (as in 1 Samuel 16:7). A righteous heart, then, is supposed to lead to "the fruits of the Spirit" (as Paul puts it in Galatians): love, joy, peace, patience, faithfulness, gentleness, kindness, and self-control (ESV).

It's also important to remember that Jesus is speaking in a Jewish context here—the Jewish laws at this point had developed numerous rules and regulations around behavior between the genders, and the way men looked at women was part and parcel of those rules. Jesus is recalling those rules, exaggerating them, and reminding his Jewish audience of the sins of the heart, not just the sins of action.[15]

What looks on the surface to be a specific, prescriptive command not to lust after women for fear of sinning is instead a reminder and a command about sins of the heart—about the attitudes taken into sexual situations and the relationships between the genders. Rather than creating a hard and fast rule about not looking at women at all, Jesus is reminding us that our attitudes, our hearts, are what matter here.

It is not arousal that is the problem, but the disordered relationship between your mind and your body—if you are fearful of your own flesh and your own physiological reactions, lust is going to become a problem. But if you are able to recognize that natural, biological reactions do not have the power to control you, you no longer fear their power. Lust is no longer a big scary monster hiding under your bed.

Myth 4: We *Belong* to Our Future Spouses

In the Ludys' popular book *When God Writes Your Love Story*, the two coauthors share stories of how each chose to wait until marriage and not date around, to honor their future spouse. Leslie Ludy writes (emphasis original):

> My entire perspective on purity changed the day I committed to truly loving my future husband with the way I lived. I realized that real purity was far more than just trying not to fall off the edge of a cliff. It wasn't just trying to *technically* stay a virgin until marriage. Rather, purity was a lifestyle. It meant living to love and honor my future husband *all the days of my life*—with my thoughts, my actions, my words, my emotions, and my body.[16]

The Ludys, Justin Lookadoo, Joshua Harris, John and Stasi Eldredge, and Rob Bell all pull on this idea that purity means we belong to our future spouses. The idea is an extension of one that we find in Paul.

Paul addresses the concept of sex within marriage in 1 Corinthians 7:4, saying that the wife's body belongs to her husband and vice versa. This verse is commonly read to signify that marriage is such a unitive force that the people involved no longer have individual rights to their bodies, but rather their partner has rights over them. This reading ignores the important context of how the Corinthians were acting at the time—Paul here is not necessarily rejecting the idea of individual rights,* but rather the influence of a philosophy in which women denied their husbands *any form* of intimacy for extended periods. Paul is responding to a trend in marriages whereby the man is denied any and all intimacy by his wife, and commanding that Christians should not act this way.

Additionally, Paul is flipping the common traditions on their head by making this a verse of mutual ownership. Typically, as discussed earlier, marriages acted as property exchanges in which the woman was the property, equivalent to sheep or goats or money. But in this verse, Paul commands that men give themselves to their wives just as wives give themselves to their husbands—a remarkable notion of mutuality.

Paul's command here, then, is not one commanding ownership and headship, but rather commanding mutuality, an expectation of respect—even in the bedroom—between committed partners. This is a far cry from the ancient tradition that men literally owned their wives and could do what they wanted with them. It's still not exactly progressive, but it is getting there.

Purity proponents take this concept of mutuality, specifically confined to the idea of an extant marriage, and extend it to be a timeless concept, no matter where in life you are. If you are fourteen years old, in the purity movement, you should be thinking about honoring your future spouse. But this is a bastardization of Paul's commands

---

* It's worth noting that such a concept would be fairly confusing for him.

here, as he is referring specifically to the state of marriage in that particular time. The "future spouse" idea is mere conjecture, made to reinforce an anti-lusting agenda, rather than having an actual Biblical basis.

But there are other more troubling themes about "keeping the marriage bed undefiled," not necessarily confined to Paul (or rather an unknown writer in the Pauline style†). In Hebrews 13:4 (ESV) we find a command to keep the marriage bed undefiled: "Let marriage be held in honor among all, and let the marriage bed be undefiled, for God will judge the sexually immoral and adulterous." This verse appears in the conclusion to Hebrews, where the author is leaving his people with final exhortations and thoughts. It appears in the midst of a rapid-fire list of things to remember, like showing hospitality to strangers, caring for the suffering and those in prison, and being content with the material possessions you have.

Many proponents point to this verse and others like it as demonstrating how important the marriage bed is and that premarital sex defiles it because it dishonors a future spouse and a future marriage bed. But that divorces the verse from the context in which it sits. During the time of the early church, asceticism was a growing movement— and this movement argued against marriage as a form of worldly indulgence. So, some commentaries indicate, the author of Hebrews could very well be speaking out here against this trend of not marrying at all.[17]

---

† It was common, at that time, for authors who were not actually a famous apostle to attach such an apostle's name to a writing. They would imitate his style, and it wasn't considered plagiarism but rather an homage.

Myth 5: The Bible *Clearly* Says
Premarital Sex Is Sinful

The fifth and final myth is that the Bible is absolutely, fundamentally clear about whether premarital sex is a sin. From Old Testament to New, the reality is far messier.

Take, for example, the famously sensual Old Testament book Song of Songs (alternately known as the Song of Solomon). In his typical controversy-causing way, Seattle pastor Mark Driscoll made himself famous with a sermon series on this book in which he discussed the sexual relationship between man and wife in explicit terms. At one point he argued that the explicit nature of the Song of Songs indicates a necessity for a wife to "service" her husband via acts such as fellatio.[18]

Driscoll's reading is interesting, because he refuses to attempt to explain away the explicit nature of the poem. But he also refuses to take the poem within its own context, which is likely not that of a marriage relationship—indeed, contextual clues tell us it is premarital. For that we must look at the poem itself.

In the Song of Songs, we find a groom and his bride praising each other's bodies and delighting in the rapture of sex. Using Hebraic poetry that, yes, sounds a little strange to our modern ears, they praise every part of each other's bodies and get fairly explicit about their sexual encounters.

And, many scholars proclaim, they're probably not married.

Textual clues indicate that this particular song is taking place prior to a wedding ceremony—with the groom coming to the bride's family home and singing at the gate. Yet the explicit nature of the material and the clear awareness of each other's bodies indicate a lack of chastity on the part of the couple. Within the Song of Songs, we find possibly the Bible's clearest expression of romantic love, and it's a romantic and sexual love that is not bound by marriage or happening within the bonds of chastity. It is racy, it is sexual, and it is happening outside the bounds of what the purity movement would proclaim as godly. This couple, the Shulamite and her fiancé, are not condemned, do not get stoned, and indeed marry, happily and romantically.

One verse always pulled from the Song of Songs appears as part of a repeated refrain: "Daughters of Jerusalem, I charge you by the gazelles and by the does of the field: Do not arouse or awaken love until it so desires." In verse 2:7 (NIV), this refrain appears to refer to literal wakefulness—it appears immediately following a description of the woman's sleeping lover. Here *love* appears to be a concrete noun—it is referring to a specific person, as in the phrase *my love*. Purity culture, however, gives *love* an abstract, sexual meaning here.

Later the refrain takes on different meaning. The Shulamite, by repeating this phrase, is saying something more abstract. It is likely that she is discussing maturity— she would be quite young, and is instructing those even younger. The message, far from being sexual, is about becoming too attached too quickly—one must approach love (and sex) with maturity, which may come when you're eighteen or thirty-four, married or single.

But the Shulamite and her lover aren't the only ones who muddy the waters about the Bible's prohibitions on premarital sexual activity. Purity advocates rely on verses from Paul about fornication. Rob Bell discusses how Paul advocates that it is "better to marry than to burn" (1 Corinthians 7, NIV) and says that Paul asks the Corinthians to "live for a higher purpose than just fulfilling their urges."[19] Bell pits the biological urge to have sex against Paul's imperative to flee fornication and sexual immorality, implying that our flesh is our enemy here.

But what is Paul really telling us to flee? Indeed, in line with his thoughts about idolatry, Paul may be urging people not to make sex an idol.

A disordered sex life is not necessarily one in which sex happens before wedding vows, but rather one in which sex takes on importance in one's life to the point of blocking out all other considerations. Sex becomes the god we worship, and we will go to any length to obtain it—no matter who or what gets injured in the process. As the definition of fornication, "sex as idolatry" makes a lot more sense than merely "sex outside of a marital relationship." This interpretation makes sure that sexual morality doesn't end at the wedding ceremony, but instead helps to create an ethic by which we can place sex in a proper position within a balanced life.

A healthy sexuality that takes others into account, that asks for maturity and understanding and respects others and their bodies, is a Biblical sexuality, whether it happens inside or outside of marriage. It does not place sex on a pedestal, allow it to overpower a person's life (through avoidance or indulgence), or let it take unnecessary precedence over one's spiritual life. This is the path to Biblical sexuality: honoring others, loving fully, and exercising restraint or indulgence when appropriate.

Context Is Key

So far in this chapter, I've scratched only the surface of the proof texts used to keep young Christians from supposed sexual immorality. Many of the supposedly Biblical objections to, say, modern dating, or arguments in favor of courtship, have developed from interpretations that divorce the contexts of the verses from their meanings and thereby open themselves up to proof-texting on a grand scale. From Genesis to Revelation, the Bible contains numerous instances of polygamous marriages, premarital and extramarital sexcapades, and complicated and complex gendered relationships.

But don't take my word for it. Study the Bible for yourself, read the interpretations and the contexts, and then make your own decision about what you will give weight and what you will cast aside. No one can make these decisions for you—you are the only one who can decide what to do with your body and your mind. I have gone through this journey too, and am writing to tell you that it's OK to question, to wonder, and to decide to walk away from the traditions you have always been taught. Developing your views on sex is a journey only you can take.

CHAPTER FOUR

How I Kind of Sort of Lost My Virginity

My home church—a large Baptist congregation in South Dakota—participated yearly in a True Love Waits program. Students in the middle school youth group were invited to make a pledge of purity to God and to their as-yet-unknown future spouses in front of the entire church. My parents had bought me a small diamond ring at Walmart the week before and they stood with me as my youth pastor led us in prayer. I pledged that I would not have sex before marriage and that I would remain pure in thought and in deed.

I took that pledge to heart. In youth group we were taught that lust was a sin, that giving in to lust in your mind meant that you were steps away from having sex with a guy whose name you didn't even know. The tales told of people who had sex and regretted it were scary and heart-wrenching. Fears of pregnancy, STDs, and broken promises were enough for me to keep my chastity locked down. I policed my thoughts and my heart; sex wasn't even on my radar, although I knew some of my fellow students engaged in it. Even in my high school youth group, there was talk of who was sleeping with whom and what they'd done the Saturday night before church. It never occurred to me that not having sexual feelings was atypical for women of my age. I had shoved any thought of sex so far out of sight that I didn't know what lust or arousal felt like.

Yet I agonized over every crush I had. What I now realize were perfectly innocent thoughts, centered on holding hands or going to movies together, caused me deep consternation over the "lust" I was experiencing. I would think, "I'm taking my mind off God!" when I felt the slightest attraction to others. I would not let my imagination get very far—when I pictured a potential sexual situation, I was fighting off a sex-obsessed, fiendish boy. I never imagined seeking my own pleasure. My own pleasure didn't exist.

I had gotten my purity ring at fourteen years old, but I had no real context or understanding of sex until years after I'd made the promise to keep myself pure. At fourteen, I was already expected to make a lifetime commitment to certain standards of purity—anything beyond first base was off the table, no matter what age I happened to be when the One came along. My church and my fellow Christians expected that one's sense of holiness and purity would stay the same, a static rule, throughout life, rather than being a relationship-based ethic that grew as one matured.

Sex in the Library in College

It wasn't until my senior year in college that I began to let myself freely engage my feelings of sexual attraction. One moment I didn't think of myself as a sexual being, and the next I did. I remember the exact moment—it was that stark. I was watching the 2007 movie *Atonement*. If you've seen it, you know the sex scene in a library. The two main characters have been attempting to ignore their sexual tension for weeks and finally have a chance to consummate in secret, in a dark library. It's an intensely erotic scene that manages to feature no nudity. Looking at the screen, I realized sex was something I wanted and was capable of doing. That was the first time I had the thought "That looks like fun" and didn't immediately suppress the notion. I allowed myself to be a sexual being, if only in my mind, for the first time.

I was twenty-two years old. I began to be comfortable with the idea that I was a sexual being. Once sex became something I wanted, rather than something I would cooperate with once I got married, I was able to understand my own bodily desires better. I was no longer afraid of my urges and my thoughts. I was able to relate better to others because the fear of lust sloughed away. I no longer had to fear the feelings I might raise in others and that those others sometimes raised in me. Had I lost my "purity"?

I began my journey toward understanding myself as a sexual being that moment in the movie theater, although I didn't begin literally "knowing" myself until nearly two years later, when I discovered masturbation at age twenty-three.

The First Go-Round, Post-College

At age twenty-five I got what I'd been hoping for for a long time—a boyfriend. Kyle and I met and instantly bonded at a book club my friend hosted. As we drove home that night, our cars ended up next to each other at a stoplight and we flirted with each other through the open windows. By that Friday we'd arranged a date. My first *real* date ever. I wore my best pencil skirt, tights, and a V-neck top, and he wore a nice button-up shirt. We went for coffee, which turned into a walk downtown, which turned into wine, which turned into him dropping me off at my house at one in the morning.

The next day we met up again, this time to walk his dog at the dog park. As night fell we went to the local lake and broke into the public park area to lie on the beach and look at the stars. We discussed everything from politics to our families to our religious backgrounds and what we were watching on Netflix, until park security came along and kicked us out.

At the end of this impromptu date, as Kyle, who was also twenty-five, dropped me off at my car, he looked at me nervously and said, "OK, this is awkward, but can I kiss you?" I smiled, and stood quietly as he approached and gave me a small peck on the lips.

That was my first kiss, my first romantic encounter. I was giddy. Within a week we'd declared ourselves a couple. Two days later I got offered a job 450 miles away. I accepted the offer and made arrangements to move in two months. This deadline accelerated the development of the relationship. Kyle was the first person to see me naked. I was the first person to see him naked. It was exactly what I'd hoped for out of a relationship. During those two months, I spent a total of four nights at his apartment, coming home in the morning to explain to my disapproving mom that no, we weren't having sex.

That was a lie born of the Christian purity culture I had absorbed. I didn't believe I had lost my virginity when I was twenty-five years old, because virginity and purity had twisted meanings to me. By all basic understandings of sexual activity, we were definitely sexually active—oral sex, "heavy petting," but no penetration. We'd decided to delay actual penis-in-vagina intercourse until I was on birth control and we'd been together for a little longer. But I was no longer "inexperienced."

Three weeks after I moved to Chicago, he broke up with me.

I was devastated.

If I were telling you a purity narrative, the reason for my devastation would be clear and obvious. I'd "given away" parts of myself, let myself be "known" by someone who would not marry me, and become a "ruined" woman who would be impure on her wedding day. The evangelical purity movement would explain my pain and heartache as the result of our sexual activity, and their moral would be to save yourself for marriage.

But my story is not a purity narrative and purity narratives are not congruent with real human relationships, even godly ones.

I was devastated because Kyle was the first person I'd ever loved who had reciprocated. I didn't regret our sexual encounters; I mourned that he was no longer there for me, that I couldn't text him at the end of a hard day and know that we'd just sit and watch a movie together. I felt grief, but not guilt because I'd sort of lost my virginity.

The Final Act

I finally experienced intercourse when I was twenty-six years old. In the wake of the breakup with Kyle, I'd reacted poorly and was figuring out how to move on. Through an online dating site, I began dating men from all around the Chicago area. A large aspect of purity culture is *not* dating; those relationships are considered "practice for divorce." But I found that dating around was a good way to get to know myself and to know what I was looking for in a partner. I felt more comfortable and confident with myself and with my relationships with men. I learned how to speak up when I wasn't OK with something. Conversely, I learned how to ask for what I wanted.

Which is precisely what I did when I'd been seeing Bryan for about a month. I was enjoying my time with him—he was funny, kind, and smart. After dinner one evening, we retired to his house to watch a movie. One thing led to another, and we found ourselves in our underwear in his bed. I told him to get a condom. I asked for what I wanted, and I got it. Consensually, happily, and enjoyably.

I was no longer a "technical" virgin.

Nothing felt changed for me. I got up the next day and went about feeling no different from how I had the day before. My sense was "That was it? That is what all the fuss is about? OK." The experience had just been nice and pleasant. It had felt good. It hadn't been mind-blowing or pornographic. And that was that.

Later, when we talked about where our relationship was headed, Bryan told me he was looking for an open relationship, and since that's not what I wanted, I said goodbye.

No tears, no fuss. He was the person I'd supposedly "lost" my virginity to, but the emotional letdown I'd been warned about never came. It simply didn't matter.

Cognitive Dissonance and the Sexual Mind

It may shock some people to learn that my virginity "loss" was not devastating. I didn't lose my ability to bond with others, and I found my ability to love increased, rather than diminished. Purity proponents assume that heterosexual intercourse is the be-all and end-all of a sexual relationship. Penis-in-vagina intercourse has been turned into a synonym for sex. This equivalence has resulted in a lot of young people in the purity movement who are much like me—fooling themselves into believing they're not having sex when they've done everything *but*.

For me, the most devastating part of my story was that with Kyle, I deluded myself into saying I wasn't *really* having sex because it was "just" certain kinds. But by the time I had intercourse with Bryan, I'd worked to develop my own sense of sexual ethics, my own view of what worked in my life. I was no longer contorting myself to try to justify my behavior as "not actually having sex"—I had settled things in my mind, body, and soul. I had overcome the cognitive dissonance that purity culture had instilled in me from day one.

Forming My Sexual Ethics

I eventually walked away from the purity pledge I had made in church. I don't view the sexual activity of my mid-twenties as sinful in the way purity culture defines sin. I sinned, not when I had sex, but when I violated my own ethics about sex.

My sexual experiences do not fit in neatly with the purity narrative, and that culture gave me no handle for defining my personal sexual ethics. I used Bryan to "get it over with" and didn't treat him as a full human being. We were both fully consenting, but neither of us had any understanding of what our sexual relationship meant to the other.

After we had "done the deed," so to speak, Bryan sat on the edge of the bed as I looked for my clothes. I patted him on the back and asked him if everything was OK, as he appeared to be thinking deeply.

"Yeah, I'm just wondering why you chose me to be your first. And now?"

I shrugged. I didn't have an answer, and "You were there and willing" seemed callous. No one wants to hear that they've been used.

Eventually I resolved that I would participate in sexual activity only within the context of a relationship in which we'd talked about what sex would mean for both of us: Would it be casual? Would it be committed? Did we want to wait? I formed a rubric of questions that needed to be answered before I would engage in sex again.

Your personal ethic might be different. You may decide you need to remain abstinent until marriage, or that you are capable of participating in a "friends with benefits" relationship wherein everyone understands what the agreement is. Perhaps you are polyamorous—preferring to have multiple relationships simultaneously. What matters is that you know how to do this ethically, consensually, and safely.

Whatever you choose, the best way to live a life that honors the agency, autonomy, and personhood of one's fellow human beings is to live a life with intentionally defined and discussed meaning. If you choose to wait, it is important to define *why*. Developing your sexual ethics is important for owning your body, and your sexuality. It is also vital to the practice of respecting and loving one's neighbors, because a defined, meaningful approach to the practice of sex, like all other disciplines, helps us to understand both ourselves and our relationship to others. Ultimately, defining your own sexual ethics and why you have them is an integral part of any future or current relationship, sexual or not.

Your journey is yours to own and your story is your own to tell. No one can take that from you.

CHAPTER FIVE

Approaching Sexuality with Intention

One of my biggest regrets about my first relationship is that I went in with a vague sense of what I wanted out of it, but I hadn't communicated those wants to myself. As a result I wasn't able to articulate them to my partner, and the development of my own sexual ethics came out of a trial by fire—with a lot of soul-searching and a lot of work to understand myself.

This is why I find it so important for young people to be equipped with a means to know themselves and to decide, for themselves, how they feel about sex. We need to be given opportunities to explore safely and to decide for ourselves what we want and what it means to us.

Right now the church in America is telling people to say no until the sanctioned time they can say yes. But this vague standard doesn't give us much to go on about how to handle sex, how to approach it safely, and what it means.

The church needs new ethics for sexual relationships. The guiding principles for developing personal sexual ethics—for defining what sexual purity means personally for you—involve consistency, health, and consent. These are what I've developed:

1. God's plan for sexuality has many facets.
2. Your body is your own. You are *not* public property.
3. Healthy sexuality requires understanding your own body.
4. Sexual activity should always be pleasurable and consensual.
5. Sexuality is fluid and complex.
6. God doesn't shame us.

These principles are not a buffet from which to pick and choose, but rather foundational principles for looking at yourself and your life in order to develop a sexual moral code.

You may decide that you still want to wait until marriage to experience sex. That's fine! *You* make that decision. Never make choices simply because someone told you what is right. Know yourself, know your situation, know God for yourself, and decide what is right for your life. Only you can do that and how you go about it is up to you. You may pray and search Scripture. You may talk it over with your friends and family, sorting through their information and views. You may simply know what is right for you. But think it through, whether you make a pledge to abstain or a decision to have sex. Both are good decisions, when carefully considered and in line with all of you—physically, emotionally, spiritually.

It's important to remember when setting your own ethics that they are not carte blanche to do whatever you want without consequence. Ethics often incorporate both personal and societal norms, and a personal ethic that results in pain for other people is not a good one. Your ethics need to be grounded in respect for yourself and respect for others, first and foremost. We have a responsibility to create personal ethics that align with systems of justice, grace, and mercy—not relying upon rigid rules that create shame, but instead creating positive ways to understand ourselves and our relationship to God and our world.

In recent times Christian ethics have been the purview of conservative literalists. Literal interpretations of Scripture have often been used to create rules and boundaries to keep the community together. But while the intent of literalism is noble, the result has not been. Instead of teaching people to free themselves to make decisions that align with their spiritual journeys, Biblical literalism and hard-line stances on purity have created cages. The "ethic" of purity is simply a set of rules about when to say no, rather than an education in how to say yes.

Ethics need to be a force for good—a system that creates and instills justice. Freeing ourselves from the cage of rules is an important part of developing sexual ethics. Rules come from outside of us. An ethical system that is centered on justice requires change inside us.

This kind of introspection isn't easy, especially with a topic as fraught as sexuality. It's tempting to simply create a brand-new set of rules to replace the old ones. But we must push to avoid this. Holiness, for a Christian, is not about following some set of rules in order that God will not punish us, but rather about embracing the wholeness of our humanity and understanding and exploring our very selves.

The Christian life is about a journey toward God. Current purity movements and theological strictures tell us that making this journey means we must master and control our flesh, subdue it. But these fleshly bodies are part of us—they inform our experience of the world and help create our understanding of ourselves. Instead of our fighting against our own bodies, holiness needs to be about integration and moderation. We must understand how our bodies work, intimately, and we must know how to hold our desires in moderation.

In Genesis, we are told that God created humanity "in God's image." Notice that this is said only after humanity is given physical form—after it exists as an incarnation, not merely a twinkle in God's eye. Further on in the story of Christianity, God takes the form of a human, putting on flesh, and experiencing temptation and life as we experience them. To deny ourselves the flesh through a set of rules is to push ourselves away from a creation that God deemed good.

Therefore, in developing a sexual ethic, we own our bodies. We are made intimately aware of our physical nature. We are respecting God's creation, not by fearing it, but by understanding it, fully and wholly. And by understanding ourselves as created in the image of God, we equip ourselves with the ability to see our fellow humans as being in the image of God too, and to accord them the respect that they deserve. Instead of laying out a set of rules so our behavior falls in line, a personal sexual ethic allows us to empathize with our fellow humans, and to lend ourselves to an experience of the fullness of the divine within incarnated humanity.

In creating our own sexual ethics, we need to take care

not to swing in the other direction and go too far into individualistic private ethics. Ethics do have a communal purpose—sexual ethics doubly so. How we behave sexually is reflected in our behavior toward people in nonsexual ways. Because of the nature of sex, we have to be intentional about treating people with humanity. By developing sexual ethics based around dignity, we make a commitment to a communal ethic of dignity. Sexual ethics are a microcosm of larger ethics between human bodies in public society.

Because of this, we do need to pay attention to the communal effect of sexual ethics when we are developing guiding principles for our own lives. We need to create ethics that respect personal boundaries, and that commit us to loving our neighbors and respecting the journeys they are on, and to being safe people for others. We need to commit to an ethic that doesn't require anyone to be intimate—in *any* way—if they do not want to be. We need to commit to an ethic that treats people with equal respect inside and outside the bedroom. A rightly aligned and respectful private sexual ethic bleeds into a rightly aligned and respectful public and neighborly ethic. When we respect our own bodies, we learn to respect the bodies of others as well.

And that is the ultimate beauty and purpose of developing these ethics. God put us in these bodies not so that we may fear them and each other but so that we may gain understanding of ourselves and of our world by experiencing it as incarnate beings, able to have an impact for good. It is justice and holiness that call us to be whole, fully incarnated people—sexuality included. We do not exist solely as individual bodies, in our own little bubbles, but as a community of people made in the image of God, which means our ethics must reflect this image.

CHAPTER SIX

Beyond Rings and Roles

God's plan for sexuality has many facets. A sexual relationship is intensely personal, and it belongs to you and your partner, married or not, committed for life or not. We bring our own sacredness into our sexual lives, imparting our own meanings to the relationship. Some of these meanings we derive from Scripture. Others we get from our life experiences, and still others from what we discuss with our partners. Our sexual lives do not have only one meaning—they are instead a beautiful amalgamation of the facets of two different lives. These varied meanings are developed regardless of marital status. Outside of a marital relationship, sex can still be just as meaningful and just as sacred. The attitudes and perspectives of the people involved are what matter. The ways in which we approach sex reflect our attitudes toward holiness and toward our spiritual lives, and it is this guiding principle that forms the basis of our sexual ethic. We must first determine what sexuality and sexual activity mean for us as we develop our ideas.

In looking at the myths the purity movement tells us about sex, we need to start with its version of the "right way" to have sex. In purity culture, waiting until marriage to have sex is the highest sexual ethic one can embody—all it takes to imbue sex with great holiness is waiting until after you've said, "I do." Marital advice from Christian sources often offers unhealthy and unwise perspectives, claiming that the Bible is clear about how much sex a married couple is supposed to have or what form that sex is supposed to take. Women are reduced within the marriage to their gender-determined roles—expected only to produce children, mother them, and support their husbands by caring for the home.

But God's plan for sexuality isn't necessarily cut-and-dried. There is no one role that each person of any gender is suited for, and when we try to apply a single standard to married sexual life, we will absolutely fail. Christian sex doesn't necessarily mean sex in marriage in order to have kids. Sex within marriage also doesn't have submission as a prerequisite.

Sexual activity, even and especially within marriage, requires mutuality—egalitarian approaches in which both partners give and take in equal amounts. Sex is created to be pleasurable, and it is important that all parties be involved, participating fully, and consenting. Sex for pleasure is not a sin. Sex without opening oneself up to children is OK. What is important is the engagement with the sacredness of knowing the other.

Within the purity movement, however, this sacredness is simultaneously deified and denied. Sex becomes about roles, about submission, about procreation—all because

"God said so." But we cannot just tell a single story about what married sex—which, by extension, means all sex—looks like. By reducing married sex to babies and bonding, the purity movement runs the risk of reducing the sacredness of sex to a biological function. Such thinking takes sex out of the realm of the mysterious and sacred and places it in the banal. It also forces people into a certain narrative about what their lives should look like, rather than celebrating the contribution of diverse views on the subject.

In a 2009 article in the popular evangelical magazine *Christianity Today*, author Mark Regnerus[‡] writes that the problem facing Christianity in America is not that people are having sex but rather that people aren't marrying young enough. "Plenty [of women] will wait so long as to put their fertility in jeopardy," he writes. He continues, "Our Creator clearly intended for male and female to be knit together in covenantal relationship. An increasing number of men and women, however, aren't marrying."[20]

In the evangelical world, having kids and being married are virtually one and the same. It's not long after a wedding that the questions come about when the couple will start having children. A husband and wife will naturally

---

[‡] Keep in mind that Mark Regnerus is the man behind a much-criticized study of same-sex parenting. This study examined the children of parents who reported having had a same-sex sexual experience, not those who were in same-sex partnerships. In an article in *The Chronicle of Higher Education* (July 26, 2012), Dr. Darren Sherkat, who was hired to independently review the research, called the study "bullshit" and commented that the flawed classification of same-sex partnerships alone should have disqualified it from publication.

procreate and raise Christian children to continue to advance the kingdom.

Unlike their secular counterparts, Christian women often aren't encouraged to "have it all"—career, husband, and children. When, at twenty-five years old, I had my first (short) romantic relationship, my family expressed a level of relief that was almost horrifying. Although I had been unemployed and living at home for six months, family members suggested that I turn down the job offer I had received in order to stay in town and work on my relationship. I should marry the first man who had come along, because after all, I was getting older.

When you read conservative blogs like *The Gospel Coalition*, one theme becomes immediately apparent: wives are helpers to the men, and deviations from this are condemned. One simply has to do a search for "wife" on *The Gospel Coalition*'s website to see hundreds of articles about how to be good pastor or seminary wife, or in which men "honor" their wives by praising them for giving up careers to be at home with the kids. This is the normative white evangelical Christian view of a woman's role. This role of woman as "helper" and as "submissive" to the man goes all the way into the bedroom.

This narrative of sex as solely procreative, of women existing to carry a man's seed, restricts the sexual lives of God's people. It places God's intentions into a box and draws barriers around what God can and cannot do within a sexual relationship. Instead of teaching people to think about how their sex lives can embrace godly mystery, we have taught them that the only way to experience God is to follow certain rules and patterns.

Quiverfull Theology

One of the ways this restrictive narrative manifests itself is in the Quiverfull movement.

Quiverfull is the conservative doctrine that a woman should not take any steps to prevent herself from getting pregnant, as that would be a subversion of God's will. Several thousand families all over the United States participate in the Quiverfull movement.[21] You may be aware of it from the reality TV show *19 Kids and Counting*. It is a movement embraced mostly by white American families and is often coupled with conservative, xenophobic politics that lament the decline of whites as a demographic and the failing of America as a "Christian nation."

The name "Quiverfull" comes from Psalm 127:3-5:

Children are a heritage from the Lord,
offspring a reward from him.
Like arrows in the hands of a warrior
are children born in one's youth.
Blessed is the man
whose quiver is full of them.
They will not be put to shame
when they contend with their opponents in court.

In the conservative evangelical reading, a "quiver full of children" is a source of power, a social necessity for the survival of the family and the Christian faith. The Quiverfull movement developed within the last century specifically in response to hormonal birth control and the demographic decrease in white American Christians—the reason white evangelical families tend to be larger than the American average. Like the purity movement, the Quiverfull movement expresses an aversion to the feminist sexual revolution; it encourages women to leave their reproductive decisions to the will of God. This frequently results in pregnancy after pregnancy; even natural family planning is considered a sin. Quiverfull theology and practice is the extreme manifestation of a much more common theology that marriage is for the propagation of white evangelicalism through the creation of progeny.

Those who promote Quiverfull theology claim to be preserving the sacredness of sex by embracing God's design for it. But on a justice level, the theology binds women by tying them to their reproductive duty and only that—robbing sexual relationships of pleasure because they are so focused on the utilitarian value of procreation.

Vital to this theology's view of marriage is the sexual role of women as procreators and mothers, not as sexual beings created with their own desires. This is the extreme end of the single narrative: a woman's existence (particularly that of a heterosexual, cisgender woman) boils down to her ability to push out babies, regardless of the costs to her own health or livelihood.

Roles Aren't Just for Women: Men—Animals and Beasts

Men, unfortunately, don't fare much better within the purity movement's single narrative of sex. Just look at this quote from Justin Lookadoo, in his book *Dateable*:

It may sound like I'm saying that all guys think about the same things whether they are spiritual or not. That's because it is *exactly* what I'm saying. "Oh, not my boyfriend. He's a good Christian guy." Yeah, and he is looking for good-Christian-guy sex. See, guys are *males* first and *Christians* second. As Christians, we let God begin to change our character. But our basic nature comes from being male. And our first thought is sex.[22]

The estimation of men within purity culture is extremely low—in addition to being sex fiends, teenage men are also taught that they are unfeeling and deceptive. *Dateable* contains an entire chapter about how guys will lie to get whatever they want. Not only does this teach women not to ever trust men, even if what they are saying is truthful, but it also teaches men to distrust their own feelings. Deviations from this norm—men who don't view women as objects for their consumption—are considered unmanly. If you're not lusting, your masculinity is in question.

Lookadoo's book exhibits an intensely low view of men as conniving, deceptive jerks who are only after sex. But, unfortunately, he's not alone in his thinking. How many times have we seen girls getting lectured that "boys are only after one thing and will do anything to get it"? I remember narratives about purity when I was a teenager. Every single one treated men as beasts who will do anything for sex—it is a necessary part of the "woman as gatekeeper" sexual narrative. Men are beasts, women are wombs—this is the narrative the purity movement sells.

In modern evangelical culture, men are supposed to be the leaders. They are the pastors, the elders, the deacons, the heads of households. Fatherhood is often prized as the most important job a man can have, but men are also required to be breadwinners, to bring home enough money to support a stay-at-home mother—because while it's not a sin for the wife to work outside the home, it sure is frowned upon in a lot of circles. At the same time, men are required to be a certain form of masculine, to be "manly men," the "rescuers" and "protectors."

Author Donald Miller wrote in 2011—in a now-deleted blog entry—that man's duty as protector meant that he had to be able to cuddle his wife while holding a baseball bat behind his back, ready to beat down any and all who might threaten his family. Now, of course, he didn't mean this literally—it's awfully hard to cuddle with a baseball bat in tow. But the odd image illustrates the burden men in the Christian patriarchy face—they are supposed to be lovers, protectors, fighters, providers—anything and everything all at once.

That's a lot of pressure, guys. And it prevents a lot of men from connecting fully with their own interests and whom God made them to be, because their culture instead insists that they must fit into a predetermined box.

Instead of encouraging healthy relationships, the strict enforcement of gender roles creates a world in which men and women are wary of each other. Men are afraid to be alone with women who are not their wives because healthy boundaries between men and women aren't seen as possible in the evangelical church. When men become a caricature of their worst qualities and this caricature is baptized as important and right, boundaries become impossible to maintain. Friendships between men and women become impossible when every man is a fiend and every woman a potential jezebel. And this enmity creates a cycle in which women are afraid of men and men are afraid of women and neither group realizes that the other is composed of human beings. God did not create us to conform, but instead to be the best people we can be, performing our talents as deeply and being as intensely worshipful as God made us. This is the freedom of the gospel—that we are free to be whom God made us to be, not confined to a box of aggressive masculinity or demure femininity.

Sex Creates One-ness

Another myth about God's single narrative for sex is that it's fundamentally tied to marriage as the one thing that unites husband and wife. Sex, beyond the propagation of the species, is also for cementing a bond—it is a consummating force that should only occur within marriage.

At its best and most holy, sex *does* act as a unitive agent—but it doesn't require the bond of marriage to do so. And the bond of marriage does not automatically make the sex act a unitive one. Whether sex is unitive depends on the attitudes of the people involved. Sex on one's wedding night and sex when one has been married forty years have different levels of intimacy, and therefore different levels of unitive nature.

As discussed in chapter 3, this unitive theology comes from the Old Testament view of sex as a transaction—consummating the marriage demonstrated that a man's new wife (his property) was up to the standards promised by her father when the transaction was made. It ensured that a man's future heirs would be his blood, and that no one else had "defiled" his property before he married her. When we declare that any sex, especially sex after marriage, is automatically a unitive act, we both hearken back to a time when women were property and remove the agency of the people involved in a sexual relationship.

Sex is a physical performance to which we add spiritual and metaphysical meaning. But the single narrative that the purity movement tells us disallows any of our own meanings.

Submission

When I was in graduate school, I lived with a roommate and we were good friends with our neighbors, who were married. One evening, as we ate dinner in my neighbors' kitchen, the conversation turned to marriage and sex. Kristy, the wife, shocked me with a small confession:

"When we first got married, I was surprised by how much *I* liked sex. I almost wanted to have it more than he did. I never expected that I would actually like it."

Kristy had been raised in a very conservative home and still believed a lot of what she had been taught. She had been educated to believe that sex, within marriage, was a pleasure for the man and a duty for the woman, a part of her wifely role. She and her husband had a very egalitarian marriage, but even within that arrangement, Kristy was surprised by her own sexual desire.

A major part of the evangelical wife's role is to "submit" to the husband's leadership, and if he wants to have sex and she doesn't feel like it? Well, a woman who says no "denies her husband the marital bed," defying God, and is being frigid and unreceptive to her husband's leading.

With a singular narrative about what sex means for women, purity culture robs them of their own sexual desires. Like my friend Kristy, many of the women I spoke to in interviews for this book were amazed at their own sexual drive and desires once they became sexually active. It is as though it never occurred to them that sexuality was something they could own and desire—even those who had been raised in relatively egalitarian and liberal environments. The belief that women should "lie back and think of England" is just as pervasive today as it was generations ago.

This view of sex as "men want it, women give it" has proliferated throughout evangelicalism to exist in the wider American culture. Many complementarian theologians, including the notorious and popular conservative writer Douglas Wilson, assert that the call of submission extends to the sexual act itself. In his book *Fidelity*, Wilson writes that "true authority and submission" are vital components of a Christian's sex life:

> However we try, the sexual act cannot be made into an egalitarian pleasuring party. A man penetrates, conquers, colonizes, plants. A woman receives, surrenders, accepts. This is of course offensive to all egalitarians, and so our culture has rebelled against the concept of authority and submission in marriage. This means that we have sought to suppress the concepts of authority and submission as they relate to the marriage bed.

There's obviously a lot to unpack here, but most obvious is that Wilson extends the submission of the wife to the marriage bed. The man's role is active, and the woman's role is passive. Not only does this erase any women who may have sex drives, but it actively creates a situation in which women are not allowed to say no to their husbands. It is a part of their marital duty to submit—even sexually—to their husbands.

Wilson's words here—which were quoted favorably on *The Gospel Coalition* in the summer of 2012—cast sex as something inherently violent. The man's role is that of a conqueror, of someone who violently subdues an opponent. In characterizing sexual activity within marriage in this way, Wilson pits partners against each other, violently recalling images of rape and abuse, marking sexual relationships as ones of strife, rather than of love and grace.

It's also important to know that Wilson's theology is influenced by racial tensions, though Wilson has categorically denied that he himself is a racist.[23] T. F. Charlton (a woman of color who studies conservative American Christianity academically) wrote:

> In addition to the fact that Doug Wilson's description of godly marital sex is violent and misogynistic, it uses language that has historically enabled and justified sexual violence against non-Western women and/or women of color on a *massive* scale. His defense of American slavery is a defense of an economy of labor that was *built* on the systematic sexual exploitation and violation of black women. In short, the language of rape and domination—on an individual and cultural scale—is all over Doug Wilson's work. Wilson's use of the language is not only gendered—

metaphors of male domination of women—but also racialized and imperialistic, invoking images of white, Western male domination and exploitation of black women and brown bodies.[24]

This exploitative, imperialistic context is singularly important to any discussion of the hierarchy inherent in complementarianism. It prizes white men and women above all others, and uses language that necessarily alienates people of color within our churches.

Many would argue about my analysis here that I am using the extreme to represent the middle, but Wilson is anything but extreme. In 2013 he was featured prominently in a round table with respected theologian and pastor John Piper. His work is published and regarded favorably by *The Gospel Coalition*, a popular conservative evangelical site. And he continues to sell books and speak at conferences around the country on issues of sex and complementarianism. His views are far from the fringe.

With such views being so widespread, it is unsurprising that even egalitarian women struggle with the idea that they are allowed to be sexy, they are allowed to desire their husbands, and they are allowed to experience pleasure through sexual acts.

The single story of sex that we get from the purity movement doesn't allow us any wiggle room. The purity movement centers on the man's pleasure, creating an imbalance within the bedroom, leading to imbalances elsewhere in life. It is important that women be allowed to own and understand their own desires as valid, as necessary to experiencing the mystery and sacredness of sex.

Finding a New Theology: Liberation
from Oppression

So what is an evangelical woman to do? The authorities—white men—tell her that the only true way to serve God in sex is to be married, to produce children, and to submit to her man. Her own pleasure must be subdued, and her own ideas about sex erased. Her body is made to serve the higher purpose, as decided by white men.

How do we find a new way? How do we regain the mystery and sacredness of sex without belittling the differing experiences of women? How do we affirm pleasure and unity and grace within the sexual act without simply creating a new set of rules?

When I began asking these questions myself, I started looking at theologies outside of the white male norm that we are often taught in Sunday school and theology classes. In moving toward the margins, I found a wealth of theological thought that took into account varying, individual experiences and offered an alternative to the single story I had been told about God.

Along this way, I found liberation theology.

Liberation theology has been instrumental in my journey as a feminist and as a believer. The idea behind the theology is fairly simple, but challenging: Christ exists not to show us our "best life now," in Joel Osteen's terms, but to free the oppressed from their chains. But those chains aren't metaphorical chains of "sin," but rather the systems of oppression that cause pain and hurt in the here and now. The entire gospel, in liberation theology, is centered around overturning systems of oppression, challenging the dominant narrative, and making visible those who have been erased by the singular story.

Jesus became incarnate, joined the oppressed peoples, and freed them from their bondage to their oppressors. Much of mainstream evangelical theology has made Jesus into an individual God who helps us feel better about the bad things we do. The Jesus of liberation theology afflicts the comfortable by challenging them to see their own roles in creating oppression and to fight against it. Instead of saying, "This is how God said it should be," the Jesus of liberation theology tells us to figure out how to live out freedom from oppression in daily life. This means challenging the stories that the authorities tell us about God, especially if these stories have the same outcome for every single person.

The first person to carry the good news of Jesus's resurrection was a lower-class woman. This, in itself, is a radical act of freedom, as women were not to be trusted in those times, and especially not poor women. Liberation theology's vision of freedom from oppression is intensely useful for minority groups within the church. The adoption of such a view can bring together the diverse community of God in the way it was originally meant to be.

Of course, this means that to be a Christian within liberation theology, one must work to liberate others, by challenging institutional oppressive structures and by speaking out against oppression. Purity theology is one of those structures. The purity movement assumes everyone is the same, that all women and all men act in the same ways and want the same things out of life. We must problematize these ideas—we must challenge the narrative that men are lustful fiends and women are walking wombs. We must allow for the individual stories to be heard, not just what church authorities think is God's purpose.

A theology and an ethic that centers female pleasure, that affirms agency on the part of women and views each member of the Body of Christ as an autonomous being who has the capacity for sexual desire and the right to experience it in safe, healthy ways—a theology that liberates us from rules—is the answer. You must develop your own understanding of what it means to be liberated, what it means to bring justice and grace and mercy and love into the bedroom. It is only through developing our own personal sexual ethics that we can begin to throw off the chains and strictures of the purity theology that has bound us for so long.

Theologies that say women are nothing more than our physical bodies—and only cisgender,§ heterosexual bodies, at that—are neither Biblical nor reflective of God's grace. God's plan for a sexual relationship is not cut-and-dried. The Bible contains polygamous marriages and celebrates sexual relationships that would be considered unorthodox today. We are not defined by gender, but rather by the grace and love with which we live. This extends to our sexual activity as well. Grace, mutuality, and pleasure create the best environment for the healthy practice of sexuality.

Submission is mutual. Sex cannot be reduced to procreation. Sex need not be exclusive to marriage. Within and without marriage, sex requires listening, patience, mutual pleasure, and grace. Sex is not about a single story, or one

---

§ *Cisgender* is a term for when the gender you were assigned at birth aligns with the socially constructed sexual designations of the genitals you have. It is the opposite of transgender. For more on this, see chapter 12.

true way. Rather, sex is a commingling of purpose, created and imbued with the mysterious grace God gives us.

While God's plan for sexuality is not exclusive to marriage, how do those who are married have healthy sex within marriage? You listen to each other. You submit to each other. You grow and develop and learn about each other's bodies—together. The development of this life-long relationship is a sacred, profound mystery, one that is not tainted by a lack of "purity" prior to the wedding day. Look at it like ice cream—just because you've had some truly awesome ice cream treats with different flavors before does not mean that you're now unable to experience your favorite flavor. Indeed, trying out other flavors often enhances and confirms your desire for that one favorite. Each sexual encounter—even within marriage—is unique and mysterious. It's not always beautiful, and it's not always mind-blowing, but it should always be mutually pleasurable, involving the giving of one's self in vulnerability, and always, always, with consent.

Decide what sex means for you. Talk with your partner about what sex means for them. Discuss what you both hope to get out of a sexual relationship. This requires a vulnerability that is sometimes hard to achieve, but with a safe partner, you will find that this conversation will get easier. You don't have to be married to have it—it is one you should be having even if it's just checking in every so often in a dating relationship. Sexuality needs to be approached with intentionality.

We as humans bring our own sacredness and meaning to the idea of sex. If waiting until marriage is something that is important for you, then that is what you bring to the table and you have every right to make that choice.

But reducing sexuality to a role that is determined by your gender and your "submissiveness" removes the beauty and mystery from sex and denies the work that God can do through the act, the ability of God to create holiness with or without human ceremonies.

CHAPTER SEVEN

Your Body, Your Choices

Growing up evangelical, one hears Joshua Harris's name alongside those of Billy Graham, John Piper, and John Calvin. In high school and college, Christian students lap up his works, from *I Kissed Dating Goodbye* to *Sex Is Not the Problem (Lust Is)*, and the latter book pushed Harris into the vanguard of modesty teaching within the church.

Harris's brothers Alex and Brett made a name for themselves within modesty theology as well, by developing and administering the "Rebelution Modesty Survey." Distributed to hundreds of Christian men aged thirteen to fifty, the survey asked pointed questions about how they react to the clothing women wear. In modesty theology a woman's body is public property—open for public comment and public judgment. In 1 Thessalonians we're told (emphasis mine):

> It is God's will that you should be sanctified: that you should avoid sexual immorality; that *each of you should learn to control your own body in a way that is holy and honorable, not in passionate lust like the pagans, who*

do not know God; and that in this matter no one should wrong or take advantage of a brother or sister. The Lord will punish all those who commit such sins, as we told you and warned you before. For God did not call us to be impure, but to live a holy life. Therefore, anyone who rejects this instruction does not reject a human being but God, the very God who gives you his Holy Spirit.

Purity culture proponents frequently use these verses as a linchpin to argue that men can dictate what women wear, and that women have a Christian duty to keep their brothers from lusting. But this kind of control over other bodies is not what these verses dictate—indeed, it is explicit that we must control our own bodies and our own thoughts in the practice of holiness. It is important to turn modesty theology's idea on its head, to reassert control over our own bodies while respecting the image of God in others. That is the path to holiness, not inordinate control via rules of modesty.

Your body is yours. You make your own decisions about it. Other people do not wield control over you, and a healthy sexual ethic defies such untoward control.

No Matter Your Age, You Have Rights to Your Own Body

During my last year at my high school church camp out in the Black Hills of South Dakota, we took a day and went, as a camp, to the local hot springs water park. The large pool was heated by nearby hot springs, and had all sorts of fun activities for us to do—with water slides, and a set of rings suspended above the water. Per the camp's modesty codes, all the young girls were required to wear either a one-piece swimsuit or a T-shirt over a two-piece. Our camp speaker came along for the trip, and I was surprised when he came out of the changing room wearing a T-shirt above his baggy swim-shorts. After all, this wasn't a requirement for the guys—most of my guy friends were happily running around shirtless.

I swam over to the side of the pool: "Hey, Derek! What's with the T-shirt?"

"Oh, I just want to make sure I don't make anyone stumble!"

Derek was around thirty-five years old, married, with children. I'd not once during that whole week thought of him as attractive—he was just our speaker and he was there to guide us spiritually. But now that he'd brought it up, eighteen-year-old me realized that oh, yeah, he is conventionally attractive. I hadn't even noticed until he drew attention to it by trying to be modest.

What with all the cases of male youth leaders and pastors being found *in flagrante* with female students, it seems fairly reasonable that a leader would want to be above reproach. But Derek's belief that he should keep high school girls from lusting after him seems a little off-kilter—as though the problem with such cases of abuse were that the younger woman is "attracted" to the man, not that the man is abusing his position of power. Making oneself above reproach by discouraging lust seems to neglect the imbalance of power that situations of abuse entail.

When you're a teenager, especially when you're a teenage girl, society and the church end up sending a whole lot of messages about who you are as a sexual being and what it means for your position in the world. You're simultaneously fetishized as a sexual conquest and told to hide your somehow inherent sexuality. Most of the time, though, if you're anything like me, you're just feeling awkward and trying to figure out what the changes in your body and your personality mean. You're trying on a lot of different identities, figuring out who you are, and for many, that involves experimenting with sexual activity.

I'm going to take a minute to talk to the teenage girls here because this is of special importance. There are going to be a lot of people trying to tell you what you should and should not do with your body. Whether you're having sex or not, our society has an obsession with making sure that your sex life (or lack thereof) falls within its made-up standards. But here's the important thing: no one can make decisions for you. And only you can decide if you're ready.

Equally important is the idea that it is OK to wait. You do not owe your body to anyone, and you can say no. You can say no even if it feels like you can't. Even if the person pressuring you is in a position of authority over you. Even if they say they love you and just want to show that love—if you don't want to, you have a right to say no. You *always* have a right to say no.

Conversely, *if you feel ready and are of legal age*, you do have a right to say yes. But you need to know what ready feels like and what it means: Are you prepared to deal with the possibility of the relationship ending? Are you prepared to experience sex safely? Do you have a safe person you can talk to in your life—a trusted adult—who can help you out if pregnancy occurs? If pregnancy occurs, do you have a plan? Are you and your partner on the same page with pregnancy? Why do you want to have sex now?

Before I participate in any kind of sex that could result in an accidental pregnancy, I have a frank talk with my partner about how we will keep safe. This means talking about condom use, birth control, and what a worst-case scenario looks like. I ask my partners when they were last tested for sexually transmitted diseases. (I go for regular STD screenings myself—about every six months, or once a year when I'm less active.) These are awkward, weird talks to have, but a mature sexuality requires these kinds of mature discussions. If you're not prepared to talk about these things with your partner, you're probably not prepared to have sex.

Women—and I'm talking especially to younger women—have a right to make decisions about sex for themselves. They do not owe anyone their body—whether it's their wedding night or their date bought them dinner. There is no exchange in which sex is owed—only the people involved get to make the decision to participate, and consent can be withdrawn. Within a church body, all of this means we must respect boundaries and understand our own bodies.

Churches *Are* a Community, but Your Body Is *Not* Community Property

Churches are a community. We are called to be responsible for each other and to lift one another up in love.

This has been a guiding light for much of the church for centuries. But the modern purity movement has warped that principle into one that denies people agency and autonomy over their own bodies. We are prevented from exploring our own thoughts on sex. Women also must surrender our bodies to the community at large, taking on the burden of modesty so that we may protect our Christian brothers. Women's bodies are public property to the purity movement. Rejection of this idea is vital to healthy sexuality. Your body is your own, and you are entitled to make decisions about it, even though it may scare some people that you do.

In 1 Thessalonians 4, Paul tells us that we are responsible for our own bodies:

> It is God's will that you should be sanctified: that you should avoid sexual immorality; that each of you should learn to control your own body in a way that is holy and honorable, not in passionate lust like the pagans, who do not know God; and that in this matter no one should wrong or take advantage of a brother or sister.

In the purity movement, this passage means that a woman is responsible for her body as it "influences" the men around her. This makes us responsible for both our own lusts and sins and the sins of others. But what if we looked at it differently—what if it means we are responsible for our own bodies and for the actions we take in response to others? What if we actually expected people to control themselves?

If Lust Is the Problem, What Is Lust?

How is a man threatened by empire waists and low-cut blouses? In his book *Sex Is Not the Problem*, Joshua Harris explains. He establishes that lust is a problem, based on Matthew 5:28 (NIV): "But I tell you that anyone who looks at a woman lustfully has already committed adultery with her in her heart." But Harris defines *lust* much too broadly. Any sexual thought can be lust. Get a boner when a girl passes you in the classroom? That's lust and that's a sin, according to Harris's interpretation of that Matthew passage. Natural, normal, passing thoughts instantly become problems to guard against. You're constantly policing your thought life.

Sexual thoughts are part of the natural thought life, to be experienced briefly and then shoved aside for other, more important, matters. For the Christian in the purity movement, however, every passing sexual thought is the slippery slope to perversion and lust and must be guarded against at all times.

While Harris applies this erroneous Christian purity doctrine to males, it is also taught to girls and women. Libby Anne, a blogger who goes by a pseudonym, explains her experience with this concept of thought crime:

My mind became my enemy. Emotions like anger and resentment were sins. Sometimes you can't control where your mind goes, and I did the best I could to clamp down on that. I knew I must never think an angry thought, must never think a hateful or resentful thought. I knew that to be truly godly I must control not only my actions but also my thoughts. A stray thought could be just as sinful as a heinous crime.[25]

Many of the women I interviewed experienced the same kind of pressure. Listen to Kay:

Being asexual was supposed to be what Christians strove for. Asexuality was the ideal, the ultimate spiritual communion with God. Didn't Paul exhort us to cast off marriage in favor of a relationship with our Lord? Only those poor souls who couldn't stand their burning sexual passion should marry and spend their shameful desires on each other. Sex was worldly; it was but a shadow of other, more ideal emotions. I was blessed to not be consumed with such a base desire.

While Kay was careful to caution me that a purity movement upbringing does not lead to or cause asexuality, it can place asexuality as the ideal because thoughts and desires themselves are deemed sins. The only way to be perfectly holy is to stop the thoughts and desires altogether. Kay felt she had achieved the pinnacle of Christian purity by doing so and didn't realize she was asexual—an orientation that involves having no desire to participate in sex—until after she married.

I spent a semester overseas at Oxford University in a program conducted by the Coalition for Christian Colleges and Universities (CCCU) when I was an undergraduate. The program consists of students from evangelical Christian colleges all across America, bringing them together to study with fellow Christians in an intense academic environment. During the four-day spring break, members of the program fanned out across Europe. My roommate Martha and another friend from the program visited Florence, Italy. Martha carried a spoon, so that while viewing the art, when a naked statue or painting—of which there are many in Florence—came into view, she could stand some distance from it and carefully position the spoon to cover up the genital nudity. Nudity was such a stumbling block that she couldn't even bring herself to view Michelangelo's statue of David as art. Such is the pressure to avoid "lustful" thoughts.

Martha's spoon is an example of a disordered approach to lustful thoughts. A large part of owning one's body is recognizing one's own unique sexuality—and recognizing that it is a part of you. Fighting and suppressing "fleshly" thoughts just pits you in battle against your own body—constantly fighting, constantly under duress, giving yourself panic attacks because you had a sexual thought about that guy on the train.

We are created as beings with incarnate flesh, and those bodies often come with attendant sexual desires, resulting in sexual thoughts. Owning your own body also means that you own your thought life. Rather than engaging in a constant battle against yourself, setting rules and checks so that you don't "stray" and then beating yourself up when you do, accept that these thoughts are a natural part of life. Everyone around you has probably had thoughts of a sexual nature. You're not a freak for it, so why treat yourself like one? Accept it and move on.

My Body—a Stumbling Block to Christian Men

Christian purity doctrine emphasizes the idea that men are aroused by visual stimuli, and because men are visual, "responsible" women must not cause their weaker brothers to lust because of their clothing. Joshua Harris writes in *Sex Is Not the Problem (Lust Is)* that "When you [women] dress and behave in a way that is designed primarily to arouse sexual desire in men, you're committing pornography with your life."[26] A woman revealing some skin is just as bad in an evangelical man's mind as hard-core pornography.

According to this theology, women who reveal cleavage or dress in ways deemed immodest—and what triggers lust will vary from man to man—are purposefully acting as temptresses, stumbling blocks to good Christian men. Amy, a survivor of sexual assault, puts it this way:

The most harmful message I ever got about modesty was at the Christian college I attended after high school. At the beginning of the year, the women's dorm had a meeting to discuss the college's rules and regulations. Part of this discussion included the "modesty talk." Rather than simply rehashing the rules that we already were aware of, the [resident director] invited her husband to speak to us. He began to talk about all the men he knew who were struggling with porn addictions and masturbation (which was considered a sin). He went into great detail about the thoughts that go along with those addictions and about the struggles he'd had in his marriage because of them. He told us about all the men he'd talked to living in the dorms who had the same struggles. I remember him saying something like, "I could go for months without porn and then one of you girls on campus wears a pair of jeans that's too tight and I'm back at square one." He blamed these problems on the women students at the college who broke the modesty rules. It was shaming and disturbing. I recall several women telling me later that whenever they saw the RD's husband on campus, they felt uncomfortable, or even afraid.

Ramona shared the various rules and restrictions of modesty she received growing up in a fundamentalist church and school:

I have been told by more than one male friend the following:

Side hugs are better because frontal hugs almost simulate sex because all of the body is touching all of the other body and you're enveloped in each other.

Women should never let men see them in pajamas, ever, because men will think of those women in bed and immediately imagine having sex with them.

Women should never let men see them with wet hair, because men will imagine these women naked in the shower.

Women should be careful how they speak and sing. If they have a breathy voice, they need to speak more forcefully because breathiness makes men think of women being breathless from the exertion of sex.

Anklets are too sexy to wear.

Toe rings too.

There's no real right way to carry a purse unless it's on the crook of your arm. On your shoulder pulls your shirt too tight, across your body draws attention to your boobs too.

Women should be careful how they walk. When their hips sway when they walk, it makes men think of sex.

Women should be careful how they sit, no matter what they're wearing. Open legs = sex, always.

Kay, who grew up in a similar environment, describes it as the "modesty police." Her sister was one victim of this policing:

My sister would come to school clothed and the teachers (one in particular) would inevitably notice that either her chest or her knees or something was scandalously showing. She would be told not to dress so slutty, and that she couldn't wear such distracting clothing to school.

Women in evangelical culture bear the brunt of modesty teaching. The vast majority of this teaching goes in one direction only. Women do not have sexual desires—we are not "visually stimulated" in the ways men are. Therefore, the burden of modesty falls on our shoulders because "men are wired that way." We are considered much more able to control ourselves and our thoughts than men, creating a dynamic in which we are responsible for both ourselves and our brothers. Being responsible for ourselves does not mean that we own our bodies or have control over them, but rather that women are responsible for men's thoughts. A woman's responsibility extends beyond her own body and into the minds of the men around her—she is held responsible for their sins.

Almost all the women I interviewed had a story related to the modesty burden and the pressure to dress in a modest fashion, not as an expression of their own self-worth and rejection of female fashion stereotypes, but in consideration of Christian brothers. Jane, a Native American from Maryland, noticed a double standard between men and women:

> In the summers, church elders would stand at the doors of the church to measure our skirts and shorts. We weren't allowed to wear anything shorter than three inches above the knee. Tank tops, cut-off T-shirts, spaghetti straps, strapless tops, and sleeveless shirts were all banned. At camp and all youth activities which involved swimming, women had to wear a modest one-piece swimsuit with a dark T-shirt over it. Nothing form-fitting was ever allowed in church. Males were only subject to rules about headgear (no hats in church) and anything that the pastor deemed "something that a homosexual would wear."

Owning your own body means that you are asserting your individuality, your personality and your own rights to your gender expression. In a church environment where all people are treated as interchangeable cogs in a machine, this sort of brazen assertion of individuality is often unconsciously interpreted as threatening. Women who emphasize attributes traditionally perceived as womanly—hips, breasts, long smooth legs—are threatening to purity culture because they refuse to hide or mask their womanhood.

And this sort of threat is understandably scary, but owning your body, asserting your right to yourself, often involves stepping out of purity culture's comfort zone. You are no longer confined to what they say you should be; you are fully your own. Often the self is an unknown quantity, especially if you've been raised to think "men are like this and women are like that." But knowing your selfness, your bodily-ness, is important to moving forward to a responsible, healthy sexuality.

Attitude Is Just as Important as Clothing

Christian purity teaching tells us that modesty extends beyond simply wearing conservative clothing. The Rebelution survey answers point out that all a woman's efforts at modesty are negated if she has the wrong "attitude." One twenty-year-old responder to the survey put it this way:

> Believe it or not, even though guys cannot read girls' minds, it isn't hard to tell when a girl has a wrong attitude about the way she dresses....If you feel like you don't get any attention from guys because you dress modestly, think again. We are watching to see how you act, and many times we are simply cowards.

Just be patient with us and with God. Do not allow yourself to attract the wrong kind of man by the clothes you wear and the attitude with which you wear them.

Like lust, attitude is ill-defined among modesty proponents. It is "I know it when I see it."

"Modest behavior" can be anything from how one sits in a chair (legs properly crossed, never leaning over) to aspects of personality (quiet, demure). One responder to the Rebelution survey put it this way: "The way a woman conducts herself externally is one of the few glimpses of what is in her heart. If she acts like the world externally, then it begs the question how much she is longing for the world in her heart."

I remember having a conversation with a guy friend once about why I wasn't getting asked out by boys. "I just don't get it. Is there something *wrong* with me?" I implored.

"Well, Dianna, you are pretty intimidating. Guys don't really like that."

I had no idea what it meant to be intimidating to a man—I'm a driven, intelligent woman who doesn't hide it. Is *that* what they found intimidating? Was I being immodest somehow and turning off the boys in my Christian circles that I wanted to date? Apparently so.

Having the wrong attitude is a death knell for a woman's chances at being modest. A woman who "acts like a man"—who is bold and assertive, and refuses to defer to male authority—is threatening to a system that makes women responsible for men's feelings. Women who own themselves, who say no, and who act assertively threaten a system that requires them to be meek and mild—which creates a slippery standard for modesty proponents, allowing any woman to be dismissed because she doesn't "behave" correctly, despite dressing in all the right ways.

Large portions of modesty teachings are centered on making sure we women know our place in the larger scheme of things. We are to be submissive, demure, and quiet. Once we buck this standard, once we step out of line, we will lose the supposed respect of people who did not respect us in the first place. Owning your right to strut your stuff, to be fully you, does mean you will sacrifice your place within the system. But stepping outside the system, being fully yourself, is far more freeing than anything the system of rules and regulations has to offer. We are more free when we are allowed to be fully ourselves.

A Lady in the Street and a Freak in the Bed

Women are responsible for being modest and not causing temptation—until they reach the marriage bed. Then the switch flips and they are required to be something entirely different—a sexy companion for their husband. It is implied throughout evangelical purity and modesty culture that a wife's responsibility is to be sexy for her husband, always sexually available to him, and to keep up her image without also tempting other men.

Prominent pastors like Mark Driscoll of Mars Hill Church in Seattle warn that a husband might stray if his wife is not keeping herself together and attractive. In late 2006, evangelical leader Ted Haggard was caught in a scandal involving a male prostitute. In commenting on the events in December of that year, Mark Driscoll said, "A wife who lets herself go and is not sexually available to her husband in ways that the Song of Songs is so frank about is not responsible for her husband's sin, but she may not be helping him either." Driscoll implied some blame of Haggard's wife.**

Ruth, a married woman in her early twenties, told me of the influence this doctrine had on her marriage: "It took me a while in my own marriage to be secure about being out in public with my husband, because we were surrounded by women who were much more conventionally attractive than I was, and according to what I'd been taught he was constantly and irresistibly drawn to them and had to fight to love me instead."

The burden of the man's fidelity is placed solely upon the wife. If she is not sexy enough, the man will wander. (Pat Robertson famously said so in a broadcast of *The 700 Club* in 2012: "Males have a tendency to wander a little bit. And what you want to do is make a home so wonderful he doesn't want to wander."[27]) But if she is too sexy, other men will stumble and she will be a jezebel. It is a fine line to walk. Women's lives are a catch-22—they must be sexy and they must be modest. And most important, they don't get any say over either. In evangelical purity culture, women's bodies are not their own.

In truth, no one owns your body but you. You have the right to set boundaries on who gets to touch you and when, and you get to decide how you dress and how you act. While we should be aware of how our behavior affects

---

** The comment was made in a blog post on Mars Hill's website in a post that has since been deleted. You can find the offending quotes on the *Huffington Post* website in an article by David Goldstein titled "Who's to Blame for Pastor Haggard's Fall from Grace? His Fat, Lazy Wife."

others, this is a far cry from being responsible for their feelings, thoughts, and actions. You did not "provoke" lust because you wore a skirt that went above your knees. The person lusting chose to react that way. You are responsible for yourself and only yourself.

Sexual Agency and the Power Problem

This standard demanded by purity culture of simultaneous sexiness and modesty is heartbreakingly impossible to meet. It destroys the self-image and self-esteem of many women in the church, reinforcing the idea that they are simultaneously extremely powerful and completely powerless. They are always at the mercy of the men in their lives, whether these be brothers, fathers, boyfriends, or friends. They do not own their own bodies. And yet they receive constant rhetoric telling them that their inherent sexiness—their womanliness—is enough to bring a man to his knees and knock him off his holy perch with the sin of temptation.

It is this supposed power that is threatening to many men. Joshua Harris writes that women suffer from lust as well, but unlike with men, it is not a lust for pleasure. Instead women have a lust for the power that seduction gives them. Harris quotes one of his readers in *Sex Is Not the Problem (Lust Is)*:

> "I believe the root of women's struggle with lust is that we want to dominate men, control them, and manipulate them through sexual appeal," a married woman from Knoxville wrote me. "If a couple is driving down the street and they both see a very

seductive advertisement, they can both be tempted toward lust but in different ways. The man might be tempted toward sexual pleasure with the woman in the ad. But women want to look like the woman in the ad because we know men want that.[28]

Here Harris acknowledges a female sex drive, but portrays it as a lust for power, not a physical urge. According to purity culture, women view sex in a manner entirely separate from how men view it. This helps maintain the veneer of credibility on modesty standards. Supposedly, for men, lust is about using another person for gratification. For women, it is about acting like a man and taking power away from him. Women who have a sex drive are constantly told that they are dangerous to men, that they are simply seeking power over men and over their own lives, when they should be giving those lives up to God.

Indeed, this division of responsibility between men and women extended to the online forums that created the Rebelution survey. I spoke to two women who were members of one of the forums that helped develop this survey, to the extent of being named "Honor Roll Members"—a fancy term for forum moderators. The women's forum was called "the Attic" while the men's forum was called "the Garage."[††] The structure of the forums was top-down authoritarianism, with men in charge and ladies submitting to them.

The way the forums operated reveals the patriarchal culture that generates these modesty teachings, the purity

---

†† Evidently the people who set this system up have never read *Jane Eyre*, wherein the "crazy old lady" is confined to an attic in a house that eventually burns to the ground.

movement as a whole, and the roles women in conservative Christianity are expected to play. The authoritarian governance that showed up in online forums for the Rebelution survey differs little from the authoritarian governance of conservative evangelical churches—the male pastor has the final say. This reflects headship theology and patriarchal assumptions—the man is the authority, even on issues involving women. Modesty teachings are not isolated but occur within a culture in which women are instructed to subjugate their humanity and their thoughts to those of men.

Ownership of one's body is the first step in a long journey in which you own and express your talents, dreams, and ambitions, not for anyone else, but for yourself alone. Owning yourself breeds confidence in that it teaches you how to say both yes and no, and grants you the final say over what you do with your body and your selfhood.

On a practical level, if you're trying to move away from modesty culture thinking, I encourage you to start small. Wear a shirt with a neckline that scares you. Go out in public with red lipstick on (or with no makeup on at all). Little, brave steps will assert your right to own your body. These small rebellions are scary at first, especially if you've been raised in a culture that instructs you that any type of individual ownership of your self is evil.

But these little steps are necessary to building your confidence in who you are as a person. Separate yourself from what modesty and purity culture has told you to be, and begin to ask hard questions about what *you* want and need and what holiness and sacredness and grace mean to *you*. The church benefits from a multiplicity of voices and from challenges and doubts much more than it does from blind obedience. Learn to ask questions and you will find yourself.

Modesty Is for Thin Women

But owning your body means opposing a culture that always wants control—especially if you're not a thin, white, able-bodied woman. If you are a person with disabilities, are larger than a single-digit dress size, or are not white, you are almost automatically discounted from the world of modesty culture. Ownership of one's body is obfuscated yet again when such women receive conflicting messages about what modesty means.

"As a fat woman," Ruth told me, "I've always felt somewhat disconnected from modesty teachings. Whenever books spoke of the irresistibility of the female body, I knew they didn't mean my body."

Fatness is shamed in modesty culture because modesty culture is focused on the bodies of thin, white women. An outfit that is perfectly modest on my friend's 32A chest would be considered scandalous on my 36C's. It is hard for women who do not fit the model-skinny body type to survive within modesty culture.

The shaming of fatter bodies extends from a strange conflation of the media and male gaze. Women's bodies are simultaneously sexualized and anti-sexualized. Female bodies are public property, and discussed as though we are "advertising." A common refrain in modesty culture is that we shouldn't "advertise something that's not for sale." But when a thick woman chooses to wear, say, skinny jeans or shorts, one also frequently hears that "no one wants to see that." When we present a body that is not appealing by white media standards, we have committed a great sin.

Because women's bodies are public property in Christian purity culture, and modesty culture teaches young men that female bodies are open for comment, many feel that they have the right to make judgments based on body shape. As explained above, men are taught that women's bodies are a dangerous magnet for attraction, so women who do not fit the mold of "attractiveness" because of their body shape have betrayed their womanhood. If what defines womanhood is "I am tempted by it and it is dangerous to me," then a female body that is not attractive to a man is not womanly.

In 2013, a couple of friends and I discovered a new blog that typified the male gaze—*Guys on Modesty*. On a Pinterest board, young men enlisted the help of a female friend to pin examples of modesty. Nearly every one of those example images was of a very specific type of woman: white, thin, size eight or under, with long "feminine" hair. Femininity and modesty, for these men, appear to be very narrowly defined.

What looks modest on my size-twelve body is immodest on that of my larger friends, and modesty culture is unforgiving of that. A dress that is perfectly modest on a flat-chested woman suddenly becomes immodest on a woman with substantial cleavage. Women who do not fit the white feminine ideal have no way to meet modesty standards. It is assumed that one size fits all and if you are not that one size, you are not womanly and are not addressed by modesty culture.

Ruth told me,

I remember thinking that modesty talk didn't really apply to me since as a fat girl it was like men were not going to lust after me anyway....On the one hand, it was extremely liberating. I wore what I was comfortable in, and I was able to form friendships with guys in which they treated me as a person rather than a potential conquest. However, when I was in a relationship I found myself assuming that my husband had to fight to not want to have sex with all kinds of women, and that does a number on your self-confidence. My husband has been consistently affirming and that's gone a long way toward healing me, but I still fight the feeling that by not being attractive enough I'm not doing my job and keeping my husband pure.

Modesty Is for White Women

Modesty culture is applied to the bodies of white women and women of color in different ways. An outfit considered modest on a white woman will often be considered immodest on a black woman, due not only to differences in body build, but also to America's history of sexualization of black women. In part because of slavery in America, black bodies have long been considered public property, especially black women's bodies. This idea is not constrained to some long time ago, but exists in our entertainment and culture today. While all women suffer from objectification and sexualization, black women receive the brunt of this sexualization. Black bodies are sexualized in ways that white bodies are not, and this is a distinct privilege that white women have.

Take, for example, the pop star Beyoncé's performance at the 2013 Super Bowl halftime show. With a performing band full of women, a troupe of women dancers, and Beyoncé's fellow female singers from the former band Destiny's Child, the halftime show was a grand display of womanhood in the midst of a traditionally male event. It was remarkably subversive—a woman coming into a man's sphere and utterly owning it for the half hour of the show. Beyoncé and her dancers did complex, complicated routines, coordinated with a large light show, and displayed finesse, athletic ability, and intensely powerful singing talent.

And what did the conversation focus on after the show? Her clothing.

Beyoncé's outfit was a leather leotard, fishnet tights, and heels, an outfit that wouldn't be out of place at a dance competition. Leotards allow the greatest range of movement—movement one can't get wearing pants and or even leggings. But critics focused on the "lingerie-esque" aspect of it, claiming, oddly, that Beyoncé was "objectifying herself for men" on the stage.

This is a critique that tends to be focused on black women, and it usually comes from white people. Even progressive white people who are sex-positive—who try to emphasize a view of sex and sexuality as good and pleasurable—and speak out against forced modesty struggle with the idea of a black woman displaying such raw power. They feel the need to read such power as sexual, although Beyoncé's dance was not suggestive in any recognizable way. It is as though the presence of a black woman with agency to control herself and dictate how she displays herself to the world is a major threat to those in power, even white women.

Modesty Is for Able-Bodied Women

Ownership of your body is even more difficult if you are a person with a disability, whether physical or mental. People with disabilities are noticeably absent from the modesty narrative, due in large part to the desexualization of disabled bodies. Women who use wheelchairs, for example, are unsexed, removed from their sexuality, and considered angelically innocent. This principle goes double if the disability is developmental—such as in Down syndrome. The assumption is that people with disabilities either can't have sex or simply don't want to, which functions to erase their agency even more in a world that already considers them helpless.

A friend of mine, Ariadne, is a wheelchair user married to an able-bodied man. She told me that when her husband and she are out, people will sometimes stare, clearly wondering how such a relationship works. Some have even been bold and rude enough to ask, "How do you two... y'know...*do it*?" Ariadne, being the sarcastic, witty person she is, usually replies by repeating the question to the person who asked.

The unsexing of persons with disabilities creates an atmosphere wherein owning their bodies, discussing themselves openly, and asserting confidence that defies narratives of disability becomes hard for them. People with disabilities are simply erased from any and all narratives about sex. Modesty culture reinforces this disappearance through simply pretending that they don't exist.

You Are Not Public Property

Bodily autonomy is a vital part of a personal sexual ethic. To develop an ethic in which you see others as human, you must first see yourself as human. Ownership of your body may mean asserting your right to say no to sex until a defined point of commitment in a relationship. Or it may mean that you say yes three dates in. For me, ownership is wearing a V-neck T-shirt and a miniskirt, because it is what I feel good in. For you, it may mean a turtleneck and straight-leg jeans or a long skirt. What matters is that you are dressing yourself for you first. Pleasing a partner can enter into it, but you, yourself, and your body should not be assimilated solely into what your partner wants.

An individual sexual ethic means that we get to know other people and their stories without judgment. We respect that their bodies are their bodies. We meet people where they are, and respect their right to be themselves, even if it doesn't jibe with our personal aesthetic. For heterosexual men, this means waiting for a woman to talk before you write her off as a potential friend because of how she's dressed. For white people, it means a conscious, continued effort to avoid automatic sexualization of black bodies, and to honor black people's autonomy. For able-bodied people, it means recognizing the ability of those with disabilities to be sexual beings, and honoring that part of their story.

For everyone, it means respecting the girl in the low-cut top who is dancing on the bar. It doesn't make her any less of a person.

You are you, and you own your body. No one can take that away, no matter how hard they try.

CHAPTER EIGHT

The Question of Individual Rights

U ntangling your sexuality from the influence of purity and modesty culture, asserting ownership over your own body, creates a ripple effect that will be felt through all relationships. It's not easy; taking back your rights never is. But making decisions to control your body and what happens to it—from deciding what clothing is "OK" to deciding what reproductive choices are right for your family—results in vital strides toward healthier sexuality. Owning your body helps you integrate your life, live more authentically, and have grace to respect the autonomy of others.

Joshua Harris, in *Sex Is Not the Problem (Lust Is)*, writes: "A man is generally wired to be the sexual initiator and is stimulated visually; a woman is generally wired to be the sexual responder and is stimulated by touch."[29]

This statement is without scientific basis, but nonetheless modesty proponents insist that the sexes are simply *wired* to approach sexuality differently. Indeed, most scientific studies show there is more variation in sexual desires between individuals of the same sex than there is between men and women. The idea that men are wired to be the initiators in sex is itself a twentieth-century idea. In the nineteenth century—the supposedly tightly wound and sexually repressive Victorian era—women were considered too driven by their sexual desire, too unhinged by the madness between their legs, to think clearly. Men were considered more cool and collected; therefore men were more capable of being in authority. When the sexual revolution happened, and women began to challenge man's place as the head of society and the home, the script flipped. Suddenly men became the sexually aggressive ones who had to guide the poor little women through sexual encounters. It was always considered untoward in Western culture for women to initiate sexual encounters, but the narrative of how people were "wired" didn't match up with this attitude until the last hundred years or so.

In light of this supposed science, women are not supposed to be powerful or self-directed when it comes to sexual relationships. As a result, exhibiting power by "tempting" men to lust is an additional level of immodesty. Immodesty in women is bad not only because it tempts men, but because it upsets the power differential that is seen as inherent in heterosexual intercourse, in the righteous power a man has over his wife. Women having power, in any capacity, is inherently evil according to fundamentalist evangelical doctrine.

This view of power and sex is by far the most insidious belief tied to modesty and purity culture. And it is backed up by the supposedly egalitarian idea that we all belong to each other, that our bodies do not belong to ourselves but to our faith community. Popular theologian Stanley Hauerwas provides possibly the best example of how the church feels justified in treating women's bodies as its public property: he simply refuses to acknowledge that we have any individual rights at all. He sees sexual agency and autonomy over one's body as antithetical to the church body. He writes in an essay on abortion in 1991:

> We Christians do not believe that we have inalienable rights. That is the false presumption of Enlightenment individualism, and it opposes everything that Christians believe about what it means to be a creature. Notice that the issue is inalienable rights. Rights make a certain sense when they are correlative to duties and goods, but they are not inalienable.... Christians, to be more specific, do not believe that we have a right to do whatever we want with our bodies. We do not believe that we have a right to our bodies because when we are baptized we become members of one another....In the church, we tell you what you can and cannot do with your genitals. That means you cannot commit adultery. If you do, you are no longer a member of "us."[30]

But Hauerwas misses, in his assertion that Christians are not to fight for individual rights, that individual stories are what make up the beauty and grace of the church's history. Hauerwas works in the genre of *narrative theology*, which is based on the idea that God is weaving a story through history. He (along with many in the purity movement) assumes here that every person is well-off, white, able-bodied, well educated, heterosexual, and male. Under this assumption, since everyone is the same, we can lay no claims to individual rights, because "individuals" do not necessarily exist.

The idea that you yield individual rights when you convert to a faith system extends from an authoritarian, conformist view of faith. Losing individual rights is merely another form of assimilation to the larger body—you lose your individuality along with your rights. This theology, on a practical level, disallows a fight for justice for those within the Christian community, instead pushing people to subsume their own rights in seeking justice for others. In direct contrast to the Apostle Paul's eloquent discussion of the Body of Christ, this theology requires that we sacrifice our very identities to be part of the larger body. Such a view erases individual fights for justice that extend from our individual rights—if I have no individual rights, how can I readily fight for justice regarding my place in life?

Hauerwas's theology places those who wish to maintain bodily autonomy solidly on the outside of the church body, erasing the struggles of numerous people throughout church history and canonizing a distrust of the individual—which means a distrust of our very beings. Giving up our selves to God should not mean that we hand authority over to earthly bodies, even if they are ordained by God. Such thought ignores incarnation, ignores the beauty and diversity of God's creation, and subsumes the fight for justice into a metaphysical quest for freedom from sin, rather than freedom from oppression. Freedom from oppression requires the recognition of the individual as a self, as a body, as a created being with rights of their own.

Language Barriers

Language is a major factor in this conflict between community and the individual. In many ways, evangelical culture is faced with a language barrier when it comes to interacting with much of the larger culture. I found this to be the case as I interviewed purity culture proponents throughout the research for this book. One example was my interview with Suzy Weibel, the co-founder of the Secret Keeper Girl ministry.

The Secret Keeper Girl foundation speaks to girls as young as eight and explains to them the virtues of being modest. The ministry goes on tour throughout the United States biannually, incorporating different themes and messages. In 2013 I attended a show at each of two different legs of a Secret Keeper Girls tour. The first tour stop was in Indiana and was part of the Pajama Party Tour. The second was in my hometown of Sioux Falls, part of what was dubbed the Crazy Hair Tour.

Both tour stops had the same basic format: open with some fun and silly games to get the girls in the audience excited and moving, transition to a story time followed by a sermon, then some more games. Then there's an intermission, and the night is capped off with a Modesty Fashion Show. It's all quite predictable and very pink.

For the first event I attended in May 2013, I drove down into the middle of Amish country in Indiana, and found myself at a large megachurch that seemed out of place in the middle of a small town surrounded by cornfields and Amish horses and buggies. Before the event, I met with Suzy Weibel for a brief interview.

Weibel is a short, energetic woman who describes her-self as an athletic tomboy. Her enthusiastic nature was endearing and comforting, and I found myself enjoying a conversation I'd initially feared. Weibel's first and foremost concern, she told me, is about the labels girls put upon themselves and that the world and culture at large tell them they should have—labels like *ugly*, *unlovable*, and *stupid*. Not a traditionally feminine woman, Weibel is deeply concerned for the girls like herself, the ones who feel they don't fit in and aren't loved because they aren't feminine enough or "girly" enough. I admired Weibel's grace and heart for the girls involved. I was impressed with her candor about the role she sees Secret Keeper Girls playing in helping young girls find their sense of self-worth in being created by God.

Secret Keeper Girls is one of the better organizations teaching young women that they are empowered to be them-selves. Weibel's sermons to the girls contain a lot of heart and a lot of her own personal story—she talks often about trying to fit into the feminine stereotype and how it never suited her as an athletic girl more prone to hanging with the boys than playing with makeup. These are all good messages for young girls to hear.

Unfortunately, language and worldview proved to be an insurmountable barrier throughout the interview. Because we viewed womanhood in such different terms—I asserted individual autonomy and she desired communal ethics—we had trouble communicating and discussing the problematic nature of the purity movement.

For example, earlier that same week, Elizabeth Smart, a young Mormon woman who had been held captive for nine months at fourteen years old, had spoken out against abstinence-only education and the purity movement. Smart told a crowd at Johns Hopkins that she had been told that girls who lose their virginity before marriage are like chewed-up pieces of bubble gum that no one would want. After she was raped, Smart said, she understood that she was now worthless, she was now that chewed-up piece of gum. So she didn't see any purpose in leaving.

When I brought this up to Weibel, we debated for a bit about whether Elizabeth Smart was right to blame her education for the shame she felt, and we couldn't come to an understanding about whether or not Smart's environment had contributed to her shame. Weibel clearly cares deeply about the ways in which women are in pain. But like many in the purity movement—and many in the wider church—she was convinced that the theology was correct and that Smart's blame was misplaced.

This kind of barrier to communication is the result of what Rob Bell calls the "upside-down kingdom" of thinking. Evangelicals, especially those in the purity movement, have so steeped themselves in the language of counterculture, of being set apart in holiness, of being separate from the secular world, that it becomes hard to even find middle ground to communicate. The belief becomes law becomes immutable fact. This is a form of confirmation bias, to be sure, but it is also the result of not listening well to divergent viewpoints, resulting in a very narrow and constrained perception of how humans interact with the world around them.

Pro-Life Culture and Women's Bodies as Public Property

Chimamanda Adichie refers to this kind of confirmation bias, this belief become fact, as "the danger of a single story." In talking about how colonialism influenced her perception of herself and her life as a Nigerian writer, Adichie comments that these stories of "how the world is" are developed by those in power:

> It is impossible to talk about the single story without talking about power. There is a word, an Igbo word, that I think about whenever I think about the power structure of the world, and it is *nkali*. It's a noun that loosely translates to "to be greater than another." Like our economic and political worlds, stories too are defined by the principle of *nkali*: how they are told, who tells them, when they're told, how many stories are told, are really dependent on power.[31]

Much of the dominant narrative of Christianity in the United States comes from those who are in power—white, cisgender, heterosexual male pastors dominate and set the narratives of theology and the stories we tell each other about what our bodies mean. This distribution of power controls the very language we use to discuss our own experiences, making it hard for women to assert ownership over their own bodies. This is the narrative Hauerwas and Weibel espouse, and it has far-reaching implications for how we approach situations that require empathy.

When giving up individual rights is a dominant Christian

narrative, it is no surprise that a political outcome would be extreme control over other people's bodies. In many ways this philosophy of community subsuming the individual manifests itself in the battle over reproductive rights.

In recent years this denial of the individual right to bodily autonomy has extended itself into the debate over contraception. The current rhetoric of the discussion is that many Christians do not want to subsidize choices they don't agree with—birth control being one. But on a practical level, this train of thought allows conservatives, via the government and employers, to insert themselves into individual decisions. It hands control over one's body to someone else, by controlling the funding and the supply. In the ethic of the purity movement, birth control enables choices that do not honor the idea of sex as procreative and bonding, allowing all kinds of wanton activity. Restricting birth control by taking away insured and easy access reinforces the idea that women's bodies are made for public use.

The right to control one's own body and reproduction came under fire in 2012 and 2013, with attempts to block the Affordable Care Act's coverage of birth control, and protests around the US. Women who use birth control were shamed as "sluts." The church asserted its right to control our bodies. But according to the *Washington Post*, in 2011, 68 percent of Catholic women used a "highly effective method" of birth control (the Pill, an IUD, or sterilization). There is virtually no difference between Catholics and Protestants in birth control use, so there are a lot of "sluts" filling the pews of churches every Sunday.[32]

Birth control is an essential component of individual sexual ethics, as planning for all possibilities is an important part of any encounter that could result in pregnancy.

It is here that communication is utterly and completely key—you must be able to discuss these sorts of things with your partner if there is a chance of pregnancy, on either your or your partner's part. Being unable to discuss and plan for these possibilities is a red flag in a relationship—if your partner is unwilling to talk about what could happen, especially if you are the one who might be get pregnant, you need to think carefully about becoming sexually active with them.

And you, yourself, if you possess the potential to become pregnant, need to think carefully about what you would do. In Christian culture a lot of shame and bad information surround unintended and unplanned-for pregnancies. I remember that in my youth group, we were discouraged from possessing contraception such as condoms or barrier methods, because planning for sex supposedly made it easier for us to "give in" to it. But planning for the possibilities is part of making a mature decision and a sign that you are ready for such activity.

This planning should include deciding which birth control is right for you, talking with your doctor about your sexual health, and learning how to have sex safely. Knowing how to have sex safely and making decisions about the future are a large part of understanding your own body and whether or not you are ready for sexual activity.

The Big A: Abortion

In forming your individual sexual ethics, if you are capable of becoming pregnant, considering the possibilities is an important part of becoming ready for sexual activity. You, and only you, have the legal power to decide what to do about an unplanned pregnancy. You need to be able to discuss the possible outcomes openly and honestly with your partner. Being able to plan for and discuss these things is a green light showing that your decision to have sex is safe and healthy.

Shortly after I began having vaginal sex, and the boy I was seeing and I broke up, I went off birth control and it messed with my cycle for a little while. Six weeks after the last time I'd had sex, my period was late, and I was worried. Despite having taken the precautions of being on hormonal birth control and using a barrier method, I still feared that I might be pregnant. But one of the things that prevented this brief scare from becoming a nightmare was knowing that I had a plan for what I would do, and that I had a team of people on my side who would help me through whatever decision I had to make. Knowing that I would be OK because I had a plan in place helped me to think calmly and carefully about the future, without undue fear.

I'm not here to tell you to terminate unplanned pregnancies. I'm also not here to tell you to keep them. Only you know your situation. Only you know your story. And only you can make that decision, for yourself. Ask yourself the hard questions—what would you do in the event of an unplanned pregnancy? What resources do you have available? Whom can you turn to for support?

A personal sexual ethic must include personal values for considering the "what if" situation. There are a lot of confusing messages about what those values should be, given the ongoing abortion debate. This debate is underpinned by a refusal to recognize the bodily autonomy of those who can get pregnant. The period between 2010 and 2012 saw an unprecedented move toward restricting abortion at the state level. Many states tried to implement "personhood" laws granting full rights and citizenship to embryos in utero. (The same rights and citizenship were denied to gifted college students born in the US to undocumented immigrant parents, when the DREAM Act failed in Congress during the same time period.) Still other states implemented waiting periods for abortion. My home state of South Dakota, for example, has a longer waiting period for an abortion than for buying a gun.

In the discussion about how to handle abortion on a political level, control over other people's choices is often considered a given. Complete strangers insert themselves into private medical decisions. In the furor, individual stories and individual bodies are ignored and belittled in the race to control all bodies.

Britta, one of the young women I interviewed, experienced an unintended pregnancy in her mid-twenties. I'll let her tell it in her words:

> I had broken up with a fairly emotionally abusive ex and then gone to pick up some things from his apartment—we'd been together a while, things were comfortable with him, we made out…we didn't have sex, but we obviously got close enough and six weeks later, I discovered I was pregnant. I was terrified. It was easily the lowest point in my life—the fear of having no money, of having this dude's baby, of telling my family, of not being able to finish my degree. I spent days praying, pacing, crying, and being miserable.‡‡

---

‡‡ Medical note: it is entirely possible for a person to become pregnant if semen lands on the vulva at the outer end of the vagina—no penetration is strictly necessary—which is why Britta was able to become pregnant without strictly having intercourse.

Britta's unexpected and unplanned pregnancy ended—as many pregnancies do—in a miscarriage. But, she said:

> I had been "good" that long and now found myself in this situation, angry that I'd been stupid enough to do that in the first place, and, mostly, angry at the church as a whole for making me unsympathetic to my own cause. I realized that the current me would not turn to past-me for sympathy—that I, the unmarried, pregnant, scared woman, now knew precisely why unmarried, pregnant, scared women did not turn to the church. I knew intimately how I would be judged, what would be implied about me, what my status was now as an ex-virgin and an irresponsible one at that, and what options they would offer. I knew that it was not love that I would find there; at least, not the love I needed.

Britta knew the evangelical church would not understand her situation and her story, but would rather shame her. Her situation would have been on public display, to be read and misinterpreted and vetted. Many in the church know this intimately because the purity movement has treated women's bodies as public property in the smallest ways, dictating clothing choices, and the largest, denying access to reproductive choice.

The Importance of Stories and Respect for Individual Bodies

Individual stories get missed so often in the abortion debate. The person seeking an abortion is not viewed as a human being with complex needs, but as someone who has not deeply considered their options. In the state of South Dakota, the current restrictions require a person seeking abortion to visit a local crisis pregnancy center (or CPC)—like the Alpha Center in Sioux Falls, which is religiously based and religiously funded. The counseling session, given before the seventy-two-hour waiting period,§§ is an attempt to make sure the person is fully informed about the decision they are making.

This presumes the person seeking an abortion does not know what they are doing or does not understand the situation. Many informed consent laws are based on the idea that people seeking abortions don't *understand* what they are doing and that once it is explained to them in simple terms, they will change their minds. For many, however, the consultation and waiting period creates two more hoops to jump through before accessing a legal medical procedure.

This philosophy assumes female-bodied people are incapable of making their own decisions, that people seeking abortions are too unintelligent to make an informed choice, and that those who do understand must be made to suffer for their choices by experiencing highly invasive ultrasounds, extended trips to a clinic, and a wait of nearly a week to legally receive care.

The legislators who enact these laws—called TRAP laws for "Targeted Regulation of Abortion Providers"—are often white men for whom the people who need abortions don't

---

§§ It's worth noting that, in South Dakota, the informed consent also requires a seventy-two-hour waiting period, during which weekends and holidays do not count, so a person who gets a consultation on Friday has to wait until Wednesday or Thursday to actually have an abortion.

really exist. They give speeches about the unborn, the babies, and fetal and emotional pain, but rarely do they acknowledge the stories of the people seeking abortions. In a documentary about abortion laws in America on Al Jazeera America, an Ohio state legislator was asked why someone might want an abortion. His reply? "I've never thought about it."[33]

Your own story may, one day, become one of those. Fully one-third of those who obtain abortions in the US identify as Christian, and many of those had pro-life leanings before their own unplanned pregnancies. Abortion providers have spoken of people who had protested outside their clinics coming in for a procedure. Even those who are prepared can experience an unexpected pregnancy—a condom breaks at the wrong moment, you miss a couple pills at the wrong time. Know what your options are, and plan for all possibilities. This may mean you want to delay sexual activity to avoid the risk of unplanned pregnancy. It may mean you want to take particular care in your choice of birth control. It may mean recognizing that there are situations in which you would choose abortion—or that there aren't, and that it's therefore worth waiting to avoid the risk. In any case, the choice is yours, and no one else's.

The African-American Church and White-Centered Theologies

Returning to Adichie's ideas, white evangelical narratives often determine how we discuss race and sexuality in America. The African-American Christian community that has embraced a white-centered view of purity is perhaps seeking theological answers to problems that face the black community. For example, HIV/AIDS is the number one killer of black women aged twenty-five to thirty-four,[34] so the abstinence approach of purity culture seems to offer an easy answer. But just as African Americans developed their own theologies over the centuries in response to their challenges of oppression, they must confront current issues from their own wells of faith and experience, not those of white evangelicals. Black churches can help their communities develop a Christian ethic that doesn't center only around saying no but gives instruction on a godly yes.

But rather than working with the communities to find solutions to their unique problems, the white purity movement instead imposes its theologies onto those communities. They assert ownership over black experiences without even blinking. For example, the Secret Keeper Girl ministry runs a charity in which it brings its modesty-centered tours to "inner-city urban" areas. The ministry goes into the poorer areas of the Bronx—areas with high concentrations of women of color—and teaches them that dressing modestly and saying no to sex are the answers to their problems.

It doesn't take much to see that the white purity movement's outreach to the African-American community is not about actually solving the problems of institutional poverty and poor education that lead to a higher rate of abortions. Instead, black bodies are a prop for white evangelicals to capitalize upon. Black people are a convenient object of rescue, not necessarily people of worth who should be included because they actually add to the ongoing discussion about the intersection of poverty, race, and abortion.

Using black bodies as props, particularly within the pro-life movement, ignores numerous issues faced by the black community—issues with solutions that are often contrary to the goals of pro-life politicians. While pro-life politicians insensitively go on and on about how black women are "killing their children" through abortion, AIDS continues to claim black women's lives. And all too often, those who support pro-life policies also support defunding initiatives like Planned Parenthood that provide needed sexual health care in poorer areas where women of color tend to be concentrated. White evangelicals continue to push their purity narratives as solutions, not realizing that getting such "answers" is like asking for a wrench and being handed a dollhouse.

The benevolent racism of the white pro-life community and the mostly white purity movement places responsibility for systemic injustices on the people who are disproportionately the victims of those injustices. The sexualization of black female bodies lends itself to a racist system of justice wherein black women are less likely than white women to have access to the doctors and health system they need, and less likely to be believed in the event of a sexual assault or rape. And all white evangelicalism has to offer in response is the "just say no" sexual ethic.

The Inadequacy of the Single Story

What happens throughout these discussions of individual rights and bodily autonomy is that one story—the story of purity—is allowed to dominate the narrative. Instead of listening, we assume that all stories of sexual experiences are the same, that race and gender and socioeconomic status are incidental details, rather than essential aspects of each individual's story. In subsuming individual rights into

CHAPTER NINE

Choosing Celibacy

The national organization Abstinence Clearinghouse is based in my hometown of Sioux Falls. In the summer of 2013, I paid a visit to the Clearinghouse, which shares a building with the Alpha Center, one of the only crisis pregnancy centers in the state. The small building is an old converted house near one of the three large high schools in the city. The entrance looks like a suburban front door, complete with a large "Welcome!" wreath hanging from a defunct door knocker.

Inside, I immediately encountered a nurse's station, with two busy nurses in pink scrubs. The nurses seemed not to notice me, so I glanced around the room and saw a sign for the Abstinence Clearinghouse, pointing to a closed door.

"Excuse me, I was looking into visiting the Abstinence Clearinghouse. Can I just go through, or...?"

For the first time, one of the nurses seemed to notice me. "I'll call up and get someone to come get you," she said, picking up the phone.

A couple of minutes later, a kindly brown-haired lady,

not much older than myself, came through the door and walked me up the stairs to the loft-esque area where the Abstinence Clearinghouse offices and store are. "What brings you here today?"

"Oh, I'm a blogger who writes about abstinence education and I wanted to see what resources you have."

"OK! Cool! We like bloggers here!"

"Not so sure I'm the kind of blogger you'd like," I thought ruefully, but I kept my mouth shut and nodded.

"Let me show you around! Over here we have lots of brochures and pamphlets for youth groups and schools, and resource books." She pointed to two bookshelves in a corner, where there were rows upon rows of colorful brochures, with bold titles reading "Take the Condom Quiz!" "The Truth About Secondary Virginity," and "Do You REALLY Need a Test Drive?" I tried to stifle my laughter, as most of these brochures looked like they'd been designed in the early nineties and never updated.

"And over here we have a library of books about sex education and abstinence." The lady walked me around her desk and in between two others to a little nook where another set of bookshelves contained worn old library copies of books. In looking through them, I discovered that most of the books had been published before 1986—in other words, most of them were older than me.

"We also have some abstinence gear, in case you wanted to get a T-shirt or something! Let me know if you need anything more and I can help you check out when you're ready to make your purchase." With that, she returned to her desk and left me standing in the middle of an open office area, trying to be as unobtrusive as possible as I slid books off the shelf to examine the copyrights and the contents. Several of the books in the "library" contained information based on outdated studies—studies I knew had been examined and proven faulty in the years since their inclusion in these works. There was nothing here to indicate that they might be incorrect, however.

I ended up purchasing several of the brochures and a book called *Abstinence 101*. The book is a treatise about the importance of abstinence-only education and the evils of premarital sex and abortion. In the book, Planned Parenthood frequently rears its head as the villain of the story, intent on destroying all that conservative Christian America holds dear.

My visit to the Abstinence Clearinghouse highlighted an interesting political conundrum that exists in evangelical America. Because abstinence and purity are considered such important values and this hard-line stance must be maintained at all times, the information available often reads like it was contorting itself to be politically consistent. Stories of virginity loss—stories in which it often seems more like rape than a consensual sexual encounter—surround statistics of sexually transmitted diseases, failure rates for typical use of condoms, and supposedly terrible side effects of hormonal birth control (based on studies from the 1970s, when birth control was formulated differently).

In pushing abstinence-*only* education, purity proponents find themselves in a position where they cannot advise any kind of ethic beyond simply "Don't do it." But "Don't do it" fails when you're twenty-five, married, and trying to figure out how not to get pregnant. "Don't do it" fails when a person encounters situations where saying yes is a viable and correct option.

However, proponents of purity and abstinence-only

education are not wrong in that one should take sexually transmitted diseases and infections into account when developing one's own sexual ethics. Communally minded ethics are important here, as taking care of yourself with regard to STDs not only protects you, but protects the people you are having sex with.

I remember the first time I bought condoms. It was around nine at night, and I'd just come home from being out all day. I was in a new relationship with a guy I really liked, and on an earlier date, the only condom he'd had on him had broken while he was putting it on. Rather than move forward unsafely—which neither of us wanted to do—we decided to pick it up again later. And this meant that I should be prepared.

There's still a lot of shame for people who grew up in evangelical culture when they're doing things like buying condoms or supplies related to sex. I remember walking up to the counter at Walgreens and trying to hide the box of condoms in my hand until the absolute last second. Despite my having developed an ethic that was internally consistent and that I was happy with, there was still some leftover shame that said I should be embarrassed about taking actions that so publicly declared, "I AM HAVING SEX."

Safe sex shouldn't be shameful. Abstinence-only rhetoric is so pervasive that it's turned even the simple act of being safe into a chore, a source of shame, because *planning* for sex is just as bad as *having* sex. Getting over that shame is hard, but let me assure you—two seconds of embarrassment in a Walgreens is infinitely better than risking your life to an infection.

You must take care of your own health. Going to the gynecologist, getting tested frequently, using condoms or dental dams, and taking precautions to be safe are all important parts of sexual ethics. Every partner I've had I have also known the health status of—when it's clear that we are going to be sexually involved, it is one of the first things I ask about. And yes, sometimes it feels really weird to pause and say, "Hey, have you been checked recently?" But my health is more important than avoiding a few seconds of awkwardness.

When I speak to women around the US about how they learned about safe sex and their own sexualities, the most common answer I get is "The Internet." In contrast to our parents, for whom information was passed quietly through peers and through books sneaked out of the library, we millennials have more ready access to information than any generation before us has had.

Unfortunately our access to information has also meant that not all the information we find is reliable. Misinformation can spread like wildfire online, and it's important to be able to distinguish between good information and bad. This is why I recommend certain trusted websites that are dedicated to providing accurate, judgment-free information to young adults. Websites like Scarleteen and the Planned Parenthood Tumblr answer questions in a matter-of-fact, shame-free manner. They offer a safe, free, healthy alternative to a lot of the misinformation about safe sex that exists.

Purity culture often functions by shaming us for seeking knowledge about our own bodies. Studying even the scientific elements of sexual intercourse can feel like a rebellion. Knowing yourself, even just medically or scientifically, is a step away from the ignorance that purity teachings often instill. Knowledge is power, especially here—knowing how your body and your partner's work together can help you both be confident.

One of the best ways to develop a healthy sexual ethic for yourself is to know your anatomy, to know how different kinds of sex work, and to be prepared to enter sexual encounters safely. Having this information can help you to be confident, both in saying yes *and* in saying no.

The Real-World Impact of Abstinence Education

In the early twentieth century, a Chicago school board leader—Chicka Merino—pushed for sexual education in schools. Her argument was that children should be taught to know their bodies as though sexual health was just another subject, like math or reading. If education is to be holistic for the individual, sexual education must be a necessary part of that.

Her program lasted a year, and she was fired at the end of it.[35]

Comprehensive sexual education began to gain more steam later in the century, but came to a grinding halt in the 1990s with the passing of President Clinton's welfare reform, which designated large funds for abstinence-only and abstinence-plus education. This kind of education restricts the kind of information students can learn. Condoms, hormonal birth control, female barrier methods, and the importance of consent are not discussed.

For many of the women I interviewed, sexual education in school had been spotty and focused on abstinence, often in harmful ways.

Clara, a twenty-one-year-old bisexual college student in Georgia, writes:

> My sex education mostly happened in health classes in middle and high school. There was some at home—my mom pulled me aside for a long conversation over dinner one night in sixth grade to give me all the gory details and tell me why I should wait until I got married.... Most of the schools around here let a local Christian crisis pregnancy place come in and do the sex ed. Most of it was doing those games and metaphors they have to show that you will slowly become a detached emotionless beast if you have premarital sex, showing slides of STDs, statistics about STDs and pregnancy, and trying to convince us that we should be abstinent. As far as I'm aware, this isn't controversial, at least at my Christian school. (At least one of the public schools had some students start calling them out for the Christian-based education on occasion, but it never amounts to anything.)

Clara's experience shows how even public schools are influenced heavily by Christian sexual education and mores—the public schools in her area had the same curricula as the Christian school she attended.

The influence of abstinence curricula starts small—a few schools take abstinence-only funding and promote an abstinence-only curriculum. Some of their students figure out how to have healthy, protected, safe sex, but many of the others don't. This has rippling effects on the state of the country as a whole. Preventing unintended pregnancies alone could save the public billions. One study of California's Medicaid family planning initiative found that, within the first two years of the program, each dollar spent on family planning services (birth control, sex education, etc.) saved $2.76 of taxpayer money. Within five years, the saved amount had increased to $5.33 for every dollar spent.[36]

Additionally, according to the National Campaign to Prevent Teen and Unplanned Pregnancy, unplanned pregnancy has severe consequences for child cognitive development and the stability of parental relationships. Children who are born of unplanned pregnancies have lower test scores, verbal development, and cognitive function than their peers. Mothers are more likely to suffer from postpartum depression, which has economic effects in terms of treatment and loss of working time. Many mothers do garner help from the government, and many raise children who are well adjusted and successful contributors to society. However, the lack of basic education about sexual health can and does contribute to the cycle of poverty in many areas.

But according to abstinence advocates themselves, the goal of their educational programs is not primarily to prevent unwanted or teen pregnancies. Section one of *Abstinence 101* states this outright: "Abstinence education was not built on teen pregnancy prevention, but on stopping premarital teen sexual activity."[37] They gleefully hold up teen pregnancy as an example of how comprehensive education programs have failed, but state themselves that preventing such pregnancies is not the goal, despite the economic and individual costs they have.

The Abstinence Clearinghouse advocates for abstinence-only education in school districts and publishes numerous brochures, pamphlets, and books about the good of abstinence-only education, making broad sweeping claims about its effectiveness. In a section of *Abstinence 101* claiming "abstinence education works," the book goes on at length about the success of abstinence as a birth-control method. The authors engage in a quick sleight of hand, saying that teens who take a virginity pledge are "less likely to be sexually active while in high school and as young adults." This statement is immediately followed by CDC statistics about how "increased teen abstinence is the most significant factor in the decline of the teen pregnancy rate"—though increased abstinence behavior does not necessarily correlate to abstinence *education*.[38] A link is missing.

However, according to a paper by Dr. John Santelli et al., published in 2005 in the *Journal for Adolescent Health*, abstinence-only education has not been proven effective in delaying sexual activity or lowering the risk of sexually transmitted diseases. Santelli is careful to note that the studies that supposedly prove abstinence-only education effective do not meet rigorous scientific standards for methodology: the studies use sample sizes that are far too small and fail to control for socioeconomic and family life factors that significantly affect the results. In contrast, peer-reviewed scientific studies of comprehensive sexual education (including contraception education) reveal that these programs actually result in a delay of first-time sexual activity, rather than hastening it, as abstinence advocates would suggest.[39]

The idea that teenagers and youth should not know what sex is—beyond the basics of "penis goes here"—is the philosophy that propels abstinence-only education in the United States. But instead of a generation of people prepared to approach sex healthily by neither treating it as a commodity nor putting it on a pedestal, we have a generation of children who think that drinking bleach will cure them of AIDS and who have completely unrealistic ideas of what a healthy sexual life looks like.

The Clearinghouse's message is intended not to help women and girls avoid unintended pregnancies, but rather to stop them from having sex. On its blog, it publishes articles speaking out on the evils of birth control and making fun of comprehensive sex education. (The blog actually puts scare quotes around the word *comprehensive*.) And, should the abstinence message fail, one simply has to walk downstairs in the same building to find the Alpha Center, the city's local crisis pregnancy center, where you get told about the evils of abortion and are urged to keep your pregnancy.

My visit to the Abstinence Clearinghouse and Alpha Center did no more to dissuade me from having sex than the media, school, and church campaigns on abstinence have stopped our society, youth, and believers from having sex. What it did was firm my resolve to address concerns about safe sex in forming a healthy sexual ethic. To develop healthy sexuality, we have to learn to understand ourselves and our desires—and we have to be equipped with the knowledge to do so.

CHAPTER TEN

Getting to Know Yourself

The first guiding principle I had to learn in my journey of discovering myself was that it was *OK* to know my own body—and that indeed, it was beneficial for me to do so. This idea flew in the face of everything I'd ever known and I had to spend a lot of time unpacking the shame I felt before I ever experienced anything with a partner. The purity movement tends to shame people for natural, normal sexual desires. In order to develop healthy sexual lives and to live in a way that honors other people, we must first honor ourselves—and that means getting to know how we function, who we are, and what that means for our future. It's not only about safe sex, but about accepting and exploring who you are, getting to know yourself first.

My friend Amy wrote the following pledge in her journal when she was seventeen, days after leaving her first boyfriend. They had had a sexual relationship she had not wanted to have, and she wasn't about to let her worth be put on the line like that again. So she was specific, she was adamant, and she thought that if she just made a pledge and promised God, she would be OK. Her worth would stay intact.

> God, I commit to sexual purity. I will take things slow. I promise not to go farther than kissing. There will be NO making out, touching under OR over clothes, sitting or laying on each other, sex, oral sex, NONE of that. I will hug, maybe even hold his hand, and kiss him on the lips with no tongue. But the rest is out until I'm married. This goes for any relationship with ANY guy. I will not go to his house when his parents aren't home or let him over when mine aren't. I will not be in a parked car with him. I won't go to the movies alone with him or be in a bedroom alone. This is a commitment to you, God. I will not compromise or negotiate it for anyone.

Amy, the young woman who made this purity pledge, was told by pastors that it was her fault when she was sexually assaulted by her then-boyfriend, which made her afraid to bring the matter up at her fundamentalist Christian high school. Amy spent years recovering, not only from her assault, but from the condemnation that she was not a "pure" woman anymore.

Ramona, a young woman raised in a fundamentalist congregation called Plymouth Brethren, was expelled from her conservative university when it was discovered that she and her now-husband had had sex outside of marriage. Ramona suffers panic attacks when she tries to participate in her own marital relationship.

Jane, another woman I interviewed, still finds herself unconsciously reacting with fear in sexual situations because, as she says, "I'm still terrified that if I have sex, something bad will happen."

In talking with friends and women around the United States, I discovered a common strain, a distinguishable mark that the American church's emphasis on purity had left. Women simply didn't know themselves—their desires, their bodies, their own sexuality. What's more, if women violated the church's purity standards, they were left feeling damaged, alone, and shunned by a church that supposedly preaches forgiveness of any and all sins—except, apparently, sins of a sexual nature. Shame is rampant. The emphasis on purity in the evangelical church—at the cost of other spiritual disciplines—has divorced women from their own bodies. It has created an imbalance in which women are unable to understand or articulate what they want after they've achieved the goal of remaining pure. Not knowing our very selves stunts growth not only sexually, but also emotionally and socially. In order to be fully human, fully women, we need to be given the space and room to explore who we are—in all ways.

When Your Virginity Is the Sum of Your Sexuality

Britta was one of the many who take a purity pledge at a young age. For years she enjoyed flaunting the fact that she was pure and therefore somehow better than people who were dating around. She writes, "I really, really enjoyed being able to say that I was a virgin. I enjoy[ed] the feeling of righteousness and purity that it gave me within my Christian circles, and I enjoyed non-Christians/non-virgins' shocked looks (or what I imagined were shocked, impressed looks!) when they found out. I felt it gave me a sort of Christian clout or credibility, and I was sure that, although it baffled non-Christians, it was good for my witness to them."

As a pushback against secular humanism and the sexual revolution, much of the church has based its theology of purity around being "in the world but not of it." When I was in college, this movement was celebrated throughout popular Christian culture. The band Superchic[k], for example, released an extremely popular song called "Barlow Girls," about young women who are dedicated to saving themselves. The lyrics draw a line between girls who date and girls who don't, hearkening back to the Victorian categorization of women as either virgin or whore, as pure or sullied, with no in-between.

Being a "Barlow Girl"—being someone who didn't date—was an easy way to proclaim virginal status and be self-righteously proud of it. It was what set you apart! It made you different! It became a vital part of your identity as a Christian, and necessarily, if your purity was lost or damaged in some way, your very identity would be in question.

Britta, for example, moved away from purity culture as she grew older, and she faced enormous pressure from family and church to hold on to that part of her identity. She moved in with her boyfriend at twenty-eight, and her mom requested that Britta return her purity ring:

> The whole incident was fraught with emotions for both my mother and me....I felt angry that a promise I made at fifteen should cause such a rift in my relationship with my mother, thirteen years later, when we were both sexually active adults in good

relationships. I felt, and still feel, that at twenty-eight I should be trusted to make my own choices and have my own faith, whether or not they are the choices I thought I'd make at fifteen. My mother would have been upset regardless of the ring and the pledge—but the ring was a tangible symbol of my betrayal of purity and a token of my broken promise. It was hypocritical for me to wear it and had lost so much of its original meaning to me, but it had clearly not lost its meaning for my mother, and it ended up hurting her far more than it hurt me....I regret that there was such a clear symbol of my broken promise, but I don't regret breaking that promise.

Britta's last words are key—the purity movement is steeped in the symbolism of virginity, but fails once the thirteen- and fourteen-year-olds making pledges grow up and start making adult decisions. Once we become adults, mature, and recognize ourselves as sexual beings, many realize that the promises we made in our early teens were naïve. The twenty-eight-year-old has different goals in life from the fourteen-year-old and we have to allow room for that growth. But the purity movement is steeped in being cool, in being relevant, and not in actually making a lasting impact on the lives of women and men within the movement—except to cause great shame. Instead of talking about sexuality with an ethic of knowing oneself and making good choices, the purity movement presents sexuality as an "always no until you have that ring on your finger" proposition.

The cognitive dissonance Britta experienced isn't

unusual—very often, women who were raised in purity culture discover that their sexual experiences don't align with the life-destroying effects they were taught about. The warnings are often dire:

> "Sex before marriage will destroy your ability to connect in a future marriage relationship."
> "Premarital sex will make you unattractive to your future husband, especially if he managed to wait. It's like you already cheated on him."
> "Sex outside of a marriage relationship, no matter the circumstances, will make you damaged goods."

These images of sex have no bearing on reality. When a woman does "lose" her purity, and the world does not fall apart, she must then reconcile the horror stories about premarital sex with the reality she's discovered. This dissonance can be quite confusing—it causes women to distrust their own feelings and bodies. This distrust causes a lot of unnecessary pain and heartache as women are forced to work out how they feel in solitude. This is why it is so important to give people room to know themselves and to understand their own sexuality, even if their methods of exploring it fall outside traditional boundaries.

Hardening Hearts: Courtship Instead of Dating

One of the main principles of the purity movement is the idea that dating relationships, as they are practiced by "the world," are essentially practice for divorce, and will lead to heartbreak, disaster, and a loss of purity. Dating, the purity movement proclaims, is a way to have lots of short-term, intense relationships, and all you learn is how to break your heart over and over. So the most pure women must avoid this by not dating at all—and yet they must still find a husband.

To that end, the purity movement has developed elaborate methods to avoid dating in the modern sense. Rather than unsupervised dating in which the only people concerned are the couple, the purity movement pushes for courtships and chaperoned dating experiences. This is all aimed at preventing a stumble in purity—if you're never alone with your intended, you can't possibly fail to be pure.

According to the purity movement, one's virginity is a gift and a woman needs to protect and care for the pieces of her heart. She should avoid any and all relationship baggage. This way she will be best equipped to approach a lifelong, committed relationship. And the way she preserves her purity? Through the rejection of dating and the embracing of courtship. Courtship is an old-fashioned form of romantic attachment. A boy, upon deciding that he is interested in a girl, will approach her father and ask permission to begin "courting" her. This means supervised, chaperoned date-like activities, and the parents have veto power over the relationship. It is basically a supervised engagement process, if done correctly.

However, this type of courtship requires intense parental involvement—which is a direct affront to the independence many women celebrate. The woman's father, in particular, has the ability to shut the entire relationship down, regardless of the feelings of his daughter, if he feels the man is not a strong enough match. Done perfectly, courtship can lead to a good match. But in many implementations, courtship leads to more disillusionment and heartache than modern dating, because there is so much pressure on every relationship to end in marriage.

Olivia is a twenty-eight-year-old woman who grew up in Alabama. Her family and church believed strongly in purity for women and that women should submit to the authority of men—to the point, she says, that "women were not allowed to be in a position of authority over a man (defined as over thirteen)." Her mother read Joshua Harris's *I Kissed Dating Goodbye*—a Christian book that rejects dating in favor of parent-authorized courtship rituals. Olivia flat-out rejected the idea of courtship when her mom brought it up—despite the "authority" the system supposedly gives to women by giving them veto power over their parents' choices, Olivia wanted to have "*both* first pick and veto power" (emphasis hers). She and her mom arrived at a compromise, whereby Olivia would be allowed to date on her own, but couldn't practice "throwaway relationships"— whatever that meant. Her family was at the time trying to implement in practice what the church demands of many women—that they find a husband and get married quickly, in order to keep themselves pure.

For Olivia, this worked. Sort of. But it required eschewing the hard line of courtship in favor of mother-approved dating, which many courtship proponents would say is "doing it wrong." Courtship is a way of setting oneself apart from a culture of dating, and it often carries with it a great deal of pride—for not following the "ways of the world" or being taken in by on-and-off relationships.

I Kissed Dating Goodbye warns against any and all intimacy prior to marriage, instructing its readers to set boundaries, to eschew all intimacy—emotional, physical, spiritual—with

a member of the opposite sex (it's always male-female relationships; more on this below), unless they are both ready
for marriage.

Harris tells stories of various dating relationships
that fell apart. Frequently the subjects are teenagers or
in college—in other words, quite young. And in many of
these stories—carefully chosen and told—the woman is only
allowed to play one of two roles: she is either the helpless
victim—her role is passive, not active—or she is the temptress, leading a good Christian man astray.

Harris tells us about two college students named Ben
and Alyssa. Ben is a good Christian man who becomes
involved with Alyssa, a girl of "questionable" standards.
Here's how Harris tells the story:

> While Ben had never so much as kissed a girl, kiss-
> ing was practically a sport for her. Unfortunately,
> Alyssa's values won out. "When she looked at me
> with those big brown eyes like I was depriving her
> of something, I caved," Ben wrote. Their relation-
> ship soon became almost entirely physical….A few
> months later, Alyssa began to be tutored in chemis-
> try by another Christian guy whom Ben had never
> met. "That was a mistake," Ben wrote angrily. "They
> were studying chemistry all right—body chemistry!"
> Alyssa broke up with Ben and the next day was
> hanging on the arm of her new boyfriend.…
>
> For several months, Ben wrestled with the guilt
> but finally laid it at the foot of the cross and moved
> on, determined not to make the same mistake twice.
> But what about Alyssa? Yes, God can forgive her,
> too. But I wonder if she has ever realized she needs

that forgiveness. When she passes Ben at school or sees him in the cafeteria, what goes through her mind? Does she realize she played a part in tearing down his purity? Does she feel pangs of guilt for breaking his heart? Does she even care?[40]

Ben and Alyssa's story is typical of what youth in the church are told. What is important in these stories is that the woman is the gatekeeper of sexuality; notice how Ben's responsibility for his loss of his purity is mostly on Alyssa. She is the temptress—she's not even a human being to Ben or to Harris. She is already impure, and therefore can simply play a flat role in someone else's story as the villain, the "dangerous one."

Women as Gatekeepers of Sexuality

Proponents of purity culture tend to return to certain tropes and narratives. There is the Purity Bear video, in which a furry teddy bear warns a young man away from a jezebel who is inviting him inside after a date. Frequently a pastor will testify about having been "tempted" by young women as a teenager and how he either failed or asked God to keep him strong. There are even children's books—such as *The Princess and the Kiss*, in which a princess's parents are vetting her suitors to see which one is best to receive the gift of her kiss. In each of these stories, the woman is an object upon which men act. Sexual agency on her part is portrayed as a woman's trying to bring down a good man— there is no discussion of whether a woman could want sex without being a devilish trap for men.

In purity culture women are the gatekeepers, the ones who control the difference between sin and life. If she lets too many men through, she is a jezebel, a harlot, a dangerous woman. If she is keeping them out, she is doing her duty in supporting the good Christian man. This "woman as gatekeeper" narrative centers men even when it comes to the sexual agency of women. In turning women into gatekeepers, purity culture judges women not on their own knowledge of their sexuality, but on solely outward expressions of that sexuality. Instead of valuing a woman's knowing herself well enough to know when she does and when she does not want to have sex, the purity movement places women in a position of supposed power where they own sex and have the ability to dole it out at will. But such a position turns sex into a transaction, rather than an exploration of knowledge and self.

Amy told me about pastors and purity advocates who often use analogies that treat women as objects. Amy says,

> They were shame-inducing and fear-driven. One preacher at Baptist summer camp passed around a rose for everyone to handle. The rose was meant to symbolize a woman that let multiple men touch her. At the end of the sermon, the preacher held up the rose and it was all torn up, and the message was basically "Stay pure and you're beautiful. Give it away and you're ugly."

In purity culture, women are never active participants in their own sexual relationships. They are always objects to be acted upon. Women who remain virgins are considered braver and cooler and ultimately *better as people* than women who "give it away." Britta writes that, in the purity movement to which she was exposed, virgins were considered to "have the upper hand" in any future relationship. People who were not virgins would have to prove themselves "worthy" of being marriageable partners, something virgins did not—if you were a virgin, you were automatically marriageable! Britta writes:

> This was a very effective tactic—why would you want to artificially limit your already-limited dating pool?!—and the topic came up again [with my mother] when I was moving in with my boyfriend, although I was twenty-eight years old: "But what if you break up and then meet a man who is a virgin and he won't date you because you're not?!" Not only was this rather offensive, given that I was taking a big step of commitment in my relationship, but at this point in my life, if a dude didn't want to date me because of my sexual past, I wouldn't want to date him either!

The End Result: Sexual Dysfunction

Treating women as gatekeepers without agency forces them into ignorance of their own bodies and behaviors. Olivia—who earlier wanted to maintain her sense of power in a dating relationship by refusing to court—did wait until marriage. But because of her lack of knowledge about her own body and about how sex is supposed to work and feel, she found herself struggling in her relationship with her husband. She told me:

I also think there's this notion of a magical wedding day where you're all pure and virtuous and then when he puts the wedding ring on your finger you all of a sudden have sexual desire for him that wasn't there before. Magic! It doesn't happen that way, and it *shouldn't* happen that way. If you don't desire him beforehand, why are you marrying him? And if you do have sexual desire for him, denying it isn't going to make the honeymoon any fun. Sexual desire does not have an on/off switch.

Olivia discovered this the hard way: she writes that she and her husband had been careful with matching their emotional intimacy with physical intimacy, but had put the physical intimacy on hold during the engagement period—they were both virgins when they married, and had never done so much as take their clothes off with each other. As a result, Olivia was not able to understand why her sex life with her husband was, for lack of a better word, terrible: "It was awful. Everyone said the first time hurts so I tried to 'play through the pain' but eventually couldn't even keep going because he could see that it hurt so bad."

It turned out that she had vaginismus, a psychosomatic condition whereby the vagina senses trauma coming and tightens up before sex. The condition makes it impossible for the vagina to be penetrated, regardless of the actual level of desire for intercourse. For Olivia, raised in a purity culture where her virginity was her prize possession, to be guarded and protected at all costs, sex was traumatic, despite her having done everything "correctly" in terms of waiting for marriage and "remaining pure." And she's not the only one—roughly two in every thousand women experience this condition.

Other women, like Ramona from the beginning of this chapter, struggle with the idea of sex as good and beautiful, when for so much of their lives they've been taught it is shameful. Because women in purity culture have been treated as objects and as gatekeepers for sexual activity for so long, they end up with an inability to understand their own sexual desire and what it means to say yes.

The idea that sex, no matter the circumstances, is a Bad Thing that requires punishment is hard to get over after the wedding. And because the narrative of purity promises women awesome, amazing sex lives post-marriage, it is incredibly hard for married women to talk about sexual issues openly or even know if something is going wrong. It is this kind of teaching that leads women to question themselves when they discover that they do, indeed, have a sex drive. And it is this kind of teaching that causes women to feel as though they are unworthy, shameful, and guilty when they indulge their sex drive (in consensual acts), regardless of the circumstances.

What We Must Overcome Is Fear of Our Own Flesh

The problem before us is at once simple and terrifyingly hard. We must free men and women alike from fear and rejection of their own bodily impulses and desires. Sexual attraction is often a normal, natural part of life, but if we don't talk about it openly, if we don't create a world in which men and women alike are affirmed in their sexuality, we will continue to have sexual dysfunction as a result of our push toward purity.

There seems to be an ongoing fear that if we equip young people with the tools to understand sexual desire, sexual acts, and what it means to say yes to these things safely and thoughtfully, they will run rampant and start having orgies on the weekends. So we deprive them of knowledge of their own bodies and shame them when this lack of knowledge results in unintended pregnancies and sexually transmitted diseases. Purity culture creates an "ethic" in which the only guiding principle is "no." It doesn't create healthy knowledge of sex, but instead a sense of denial and delayed gratification. It puts the current generation of children more at risk for problematic and risky behavior.

Instead, our healthy sexual ethic needs to start with the freedom to know ourselves. This may include, yes, masturbation, but it also includes not policing our thoughts constantly in the hope of ridding ourselves of natural, normal sexual attractions. It involves placing our desires into perspective as just another appetite among the myriad appetites our bodies have. Accepting who we are and understanding that we are not freaks or weirdos because of our bodies' reactions to basic life. We are humans, and our bodies are important to our experience of the world. Knowing and understanding that will help us to know and understand our very selves.

CHAPTER ELEVEN

Yes Means Yes: Healthy Boundaries Mean Healthy Lives

"C an you give Grandpa a kiss?"

"Noooo."

"Oh, come on. Come over and give me a kiss. You should listen to your grandpa."

I sat quietly, watching the toddler being cajoled into giving affection she didn't want to, and thought about whether or not I should say something. Ultimately deciding not to, I watched her trot over and give her grandfather a quick peck on the cheek. It's not my place to say anything, I tell myself, as the little girl's no is disrespected again and again.

The socialization of women begins young. I'm in the middle of the age group of an extended family including approximately forty-five first and second cousins. I've seen a lot of my relatives grow up. And I've never once seen anyone begging a boy child for a kiss the way they do with the girls.

We teach little girls that saying no is bad, that asserting themselves in a maybe-not-so-kind way is an easy way to lose friends and alienate people. And then we're surprised when they grow up and can't tell people no, even and especially when they should. And somehow we're surprised when their no isn't respected.

According to the Rape, Abuse and Incest National Network (RAINN), one in six women will be sexually assaulted in her lifetime. For college-age women, the number increases to one in four. A shockingly low number of these rapes will result in conviction for a rapist, and frequently, when a woman brings charges, she will have to face questions about her sexual history, how much she'd had to drink, and how she was dressed. Somehow the victim's history and behavior are considered mitigating factors to a pure and simple truth: a person has been violated against their will.

One of the most important principles of a healthy sexuality—if not the most important—is that sexual activity must be consensual. Sexual activity that is coerced, forced, or otherwise performed without the enthusiastic consent of both partners must be condemned as beyond the pale. Unfortunately, because of the culture in which we live, and to which the purity movement contributes, sexual assault and rape are not always seen as such.

What Is Rape Culture?

Rape culture is a feminist term for a culture that implicitly and explicitly minimizes the trauma of rape and creates an environment in which rape and sexual assault are acceptable. This may be through the treatment of bodies as public property, or through other aspects of popular culture that go unchallenged.

Yale fraternity students chanting "No means yes and yes means anal!" is rape culture.[41]

Romantic comedies perpetuating the meme that "wearing them down until they say yes" is romantic and loving is rape culture.

A Super Bowl–winning football player who traps a woman in his hotel room, rapes her, and doesn't get charged because "most girls would feel lucky to get to have sex with someone like [him]" is rape culture.[42]

A rapist confessing to his crimes anonymously online and then being congratulated by commenters for his "honesty" and "openness" so that "we can see the manipulation now" is rape culture.[43]

You, and Only You, Have the Ability to Say Yes or No for Yourself

Purity culture leads to a lack of education about consent, about yes meaning yes and no meaning no. We pin a woman's worth on whether not someone has "boldly gone there." All of this adds up to a culture in which women are no longer human beings, but objects that need to be told what to know, where to go, and how to act. It's no wonder that almost every woman you speak to will have a story about that one time when she had to run away, that one time when she feared for her life. It's no wonder women feel the need to arm themselves against attackers. It's no wonder that many women are left without the tools to identify sexual assault because they don't have a clue what consent looks like.

It's no wonder, because we've made it clear, through the

ways in which we teach about consent within the church, the way we prize virginity as a precious gift for our husbands, the shame we heap upon women who don't conform—we've made it clear that women are simultaneously public property and completely alone.

And that needs to change. And it can change if both men and women insist on a standard of enthusiastic consent in all their sexual encounters. We need to commit to not trying to talk our partners into sex, or pressuring them emotionally or socially. We need to commit to interrogating our own sexual desires and figuring out what it means for us to say yes. We need to commit to respecting our partner's no, and to expecting the same respect from others. In moving forward in creating a healthy sexuality for ourselves and those around us, it is vital that we commit to having sex that is consensual and pleasurable for both parties involved. This is absolutely, fundamentally nonnegotiable.

Power, Purity, and Rape: Controlling Women

The purity movement feeds into this cultural acceptance of rape with the narratives that are told about sex. Sex becomes a matter of "either you have or you haven't" rather than a matter of choice and consent. The narratives surrounding purity are so lacking in consent education that many times stories of rape are passed off as dealing with "loss of purity" and never examined beyond how they affect a person's purity. As a result, many women deal with added shame and guilt after an assault.

Within the purity movement, virginity is presented as

the be-all and end-all of a woman's worth. When that virginity is "lost" or "stolen" through force, many women must deal with the concept of being impure or unclean, rather than seeing that they are not at fault and have not lost their worth.

Like secular culture, church environments are affected by rape culture. Purity culture often benefits from rape culture. In rape culture, women are punished for failure to behave properly. Purity culture punishes women for failure to perform femininity properly. The two form a mutually beneficial relationship, in which rape functions as a consequence for women who step outside the box of femininity. Unfeminine women, in purity culture and in rape culture, are punished for their sins. The interrogations that victims and survivors face about their behavior are often about making sure they were the "perfect victim"—that they didn't drink, they didn't wear a short skirt, they weren't purposefully alone with the rapist, they were virgins.

In evangelical narratives, when rape is addressed, it is a problem solely of the secular culture—never of the church. The Abstinence Clearinghouse draws a direct line between rape and loss of self-control caused by hedonistic, sexually open culture. In a section of their *Abstinence 101* text, the authors discuss the "emotional consequences" of premarital sex. They write that it is the divorcing of sex from love and commitment that causes rape:

> In a 1988 survey of students in grades six through nine, the Rhode Island Rape Crisis Center found that two of three boys and 49 percent of girls said it was "acceptable for a man to force sex on a woman if they have been dating for six months or more." In view

of attitudes like these, it's easy to understand why date rape has become such a widespread problem.

In short, sex that isn't tied to love and commitment undermines characters by subverting self-control, respect and responsibility. If left unchecked, sexual desires and impulses easily run amok and lead to habits of hedonism and using others for one's personal pleasure.[44]

For Purity Culture, Rape Only Happens Within Certain Narratives

For conservative evangelicals, rape is based on loss of self-control and on encouragement from a hedonistic and permissive sexual culture. This completely erases the incidence of rape within marriage and what rapists themselves have had to say. Often rape is imagined as a stranger in a dark alley who attacks with great violence.

But rapists aren't fictional night terrors that scare small children in their beds, easily identifiable by some physical feature like a tail or horns. No, the vast majority of rapes are committed by someone known to the victim, most often inside a home that belongs to one of them. Rapists are our brothers, our fathers, our pastors, our husbands, our cousins, our friends. They look and sound and feel like your average, everyday person.

As a culture, though, when we promote the "stranger in a dark alley" narrative, it makes us feel that we can protect ourselves from rape, if we just don't act like "those people." If rape has a specific, defined narrative with specific, defined elements, then women just need to not do certain things and they'll be safe.

This is how the church is implicated in rape culture. Because we, as a church and as a culture, believe certain myths about how rape happens and what rape looks like, we end up punishing victims for their failure to follow the prescribed rules that come from these myths. Victim-blaming assumes that there is something the victim could have done to get out of the situation, that there is something they could have done to prevent the assault, or that there is something they need to apologize for. Victim-blaming and rape culture are intimately tied together. Both dehumanize the victim and treat the rapist as an unstoppable force. It is up to us, as potential victims, to get out of the way.

Amy, whom you know from previous chapters, struggled with this concept after experiencing an abusive relationship wherein her abuser was enabled by members from their church. John (name changed) would assert himself in physical ways over Amy—grabbing her from behind and then blaming her for being "too attractive" when she protested. If she was dressed "too immodestly," it would lead to unwanted advances. "Too frumpy," and he would resort to degrading verbal abuse.

Amy's father expressed concern about John to the pastors of the church. Their reply? "You need to trust John because he's a Christian."

Eventually Amy gave in to John's advances. Since she had consented once and was now "impure," John used that against her. "You're not a virgin anymore, so you might as well" was the message used to pressure her into a sexual relationship she did not want and had not consented to.

This was something she didn't identify as rape because it was how she was raised to view sexual relationships. She writes:

> Rape was often used as a scare tactic at my first church. Some actual examples: If you went too far with a guy you might "get raped." If you dressed too scantily, you might "get raped." If you drank alcohol or went to a club, you might "get raped." If you went to a public university you might "get raped."... Church and school were so highly concerned with reputation, that I would have been afraid of being silenced or blamed.

Amy's story is not unusual in the least. In fact, it's similar to those of many of the women I interviewed.

The Stories We Tell About "Virginity Loss" Are Often Really About Rape

Challenging the way we talk about rape requires that we, as a church culture, examine our rhetoric and the ways in which we teach our children about consent and respect for women's bodies. It's hard work. Many of the narratives about loss of purity that are common in evangelical culture are stories of rape. For example, in numerous stories told within the *Abstinence 101* text, a woman is actively pressured into having sex by a boyfriend, and her subsequent trauma at being raped is held up as the result of premarital sex. At one point the authors tell the following story of a young woman:

With each date, my boyfriend's requests for sex became more convincing. After all, we did love each other. Within two months, I gave in, because I had justified the whole thing. Over the next six months, sex became the center of our relationship....At the same time, some new things entered our relationship—things like anger, impatience, jealousy, and selfishness. We just couldn't talk anymore. We grew very bored with each other. I desperately wanted a change.[45]

Once again, what the young lady is describing is rape—she "gave in" to her boyfriend's pressure. A relationship with someone who pressures you into having sex—who rapes you—isn't going to be healthy. But, according to the Abstinence Clearinghouse's framing of the issue, the problem here is not that the sex was done in a coercive, unhealthy manner, but that the sex happened at all.

Such a story, in a healthy environment, should be a lesson about consent—coerced sex is not sex, but rape. Instead of a springboard for discussing consent, however, evangelical leaders and purity proponents see this kind of story as a means to warn people against sex altogether. Instead of teaching how to tell the difference between a no and a yes, and making it clear what consent is, evangelical culture often uses the trauma of rape to explain why no one should ever say yes. At least, no one should say yes until marriage.

Relatedly, blogger and evangelical author Cory Copeland offered a prototype of a victim-blaming narrative on his blog, posted in June 2012:

There was once a girl who lived her life the way a good girl should. She was meek and humble, and she did all she could for those in need around her.... This girl met a boy and that boy had a way about him.... He captured the good girl in his madness and she soon fell in the deepest of love. The girl held strong at first, tossing away her boy's hands as they searched her body, seeking satisfaction. Again and again, she dissuaded him, turning a stone cold cheek and halting heavy breaths before they pushed too far. But the boy was relentless and vile in his objections to her goodness. He bombarded her wits with fallacies of unrequited love and lacking attention.... Soon, the good girl could take no more, so she stripped herself of the righteousness she held so close and took the boy into her bed.[46]

What is described is an abusive situation, a coerced sexual relationship. But it is never identified as abusive. Indeed, Copeland's conclusion to the story is telling—after this rape (which Copeland does not identify as such), the girl is broken and confused, and falls "to those things she had always resisted."

According to Copeland's narrative, "She was lost in her abandonment and she didn't want to be found. She did what she wanted with whomever she wished.... The once good girl was now void of any goodness." He closes his piece with a call to forgiveness, explaining that all the girl need do now is seek forgiveness for her crimes of passion, and she will be set free.

There are two things that should be noted in this situation. The first is that a woman who seeks after and delights in sex is portrayed as somehow void of any and all goodness—her righteousness is given up, stripped from her, the moment she takes agency in having sex, which this girl presumably did following her rape.

The second is that all-important word—*rape*. This is the narrative of "forbidden fruit" many evangelical women are sold—once a woman experiences sex, she will stop at nothing to get more because she wants to feel that closeness over and over. But these narratives, as in Copeland's example, often talk about sex that was not consensual, that was coerced. The abusive nature of the relationship is never acknowledged, never seen for what it is. Instead, a girl who could resist no longer, a girl who gave in, is cast as having *voluntarily* given up that which should be most precious to her. That is a major problem—her consent was not given freely, but was coerced and pulled from her, which makes it not consent at all.

American evangelical culture doesn't recognize this.

"You Can Turn Me On, But Don't Expect Me to Respect You."

The evangelical definitions of rape and explanations for it feed off and feed into secular narratives about how rape happens. A patriarchal attitude toward women—amplified and given legitimacy by "Bible-believing pastors"—only serves to create leniency toward rape and forgiveness for rapists.

Evangelical culture is fueled by an industry built around promoting "proper" and "godly" ways to date and engage in relationships. Dating and Christian living guides for men and women that address rape often do so in ways that are unhelpful toward victims and survivors of rape. Take John and Stasi Eldredge's best-selling book *Captivating*. In this book Stasi Eldredge says that rape is bad, but that it is also the response of Satan to a woman who is living in God's beauty. She theologizes rape as the inevitable consequence for a woman who is being who God called her to be. This creates the message that women who are living as God wants them to should expect to get raped. Because Satan.

In other dating guides, rape is a punishment not for being godly, but for a failure to be so. Numerous dating guides are filled with rhetoric that blames the victim. Take for example the Christian dating guide *Dateable*, by Justin Lookadoo and Hayley DiMarco. The book starts with some depressing gender essentialism, with the authors declaring that men really don't think about marriage and women are planning their weddings from childhood. It then goes into why you should hold back physically in a relationship, especially as a woman, saying,

> Sex creates a soul connection. It doesn't matter if you want it to or not. God created it that way. So the more you give up sexually in a relationship, the more it rips your soul apart. It creates scars that will never go away. Plus, you become a number.[47]

Aside from the intense nihilism shown about dating relationships (the first chapter is titled "It Will Not Last"), the book begins to reinforce rape culture overtly and intensely as it goes on. When it comes to how guys view women, it gets disturbing. First Lookadoo talks about how girls who dress as if they are "EZ" probably are. Then there's this gem:

> When you put on that little babydoll tee showing all your business, every guy from 8 to 80 is staring at you. Oh, I know, "It's fashion. That's what I look good in." That's not the point! Your target is teenage guys. You are trying to get them to notice you. But that's not what's happening. . . . Every man is staring at you. When you wear those tight little shorts, every man is staring at your butt. When you wear the tight, revealing shirt, every guy is looking at your breasts. Think about your grandfather, because all his old friends are looking at your breasts when you wear that stuff. Eww! I know it's gross, but that's the truth. *If you dress like a piece of meat, you're gonna get thrown on the BBQ. It's that simple.*[48]

It's really hard not to see that last line as a threat of sexual violence—the concept of being "thrown on the BBQ" is an inherently violent one. It's a situation that doesn't end well for the woman, and is seen as the direct result of her dress. But the thing is, much of evangelical culture feels justified in using the threat of sexual violence in response to women who step outside their gendered boxes. Respect for a woman's body and her consent is considered conditional upon whether or not she is being feminine enough.

Lookadoo isn't alone in using language that threatens rape or loss of respect based on the perceived sexuality of a woman. In the Rebelution survey mentioned in chapter 7, the Harris brothers posed a question: "How do you feel about girls who purposely flaunt their bodies?" The responses revealed a lot about how men in evangelical culture speak about women:

> It is hard for me to respect them. I love them, and pray that God might save them, if they are lost, and sanctify those whom He has called but I do have a sense of dislike toward them because of how hard they make life for me. Our lives are to be lived in a way that glorifies God, that is no way glorifying Him or making me better able to glorify Him. [Age 23]

> Yes, you can turn me on, but don't expect me to respect you. Yes, I might find you attractive on the outside, but that won't make me think of you as attractive on the inside. Sure you might get my attention, but it will be negative attention. [Age 35–39]

> If you flaunt yourself, you have the attention of lots of guys, but you instantly lose their respect and admiration. [Age 17]

> When a girl is flaunting her body, my opinion of her character lowers quite a bit. I get the strong impression that she does not respect Biblical standards of modesty and purity, or the Biblical injunctions to avoid causing your brothers in Christ to sin. [Age 17]

Women are not fully human in the minds of these men because they are objects for temptation. If women choose to act in a way that does not conform to a certain man's idea of Biblical standards, basic dignity and respect are forfeit. And if basic dignity and respect are forfeit, the women's bodies themselves don't matter, placing these women in the category of "asking for it" if/when they encounter a rapist.

Other popular evangelical voices contribute to this idea that rape can somehow be the fault of the victim. Often, when confronted about this victim-blaming, pastors and purity movement proponents will protest that they, personally, *hate* rape, so they couldn't possibly be contributing to a culture that supports it. Douglas Wilson, conservative complementarian writer, responded to the idea that complementarians support rape culture in a blog post titled "A Tall Tree, and a Short Rope"***:

> So do I believe that if some girl goes to a frat party with a hardened resolve to drink way too much, with a t-shirt on that says "No Means No," but after three beers she takes that shirt off because all the boys wanted her to, and then the next thing she knows she wakes up in the morning having been raped…do I somehow believe that is not rape? No, of course it is rape. It is the rape of a dope, but it is still a rape.[49]

Wilson seems to be under the impression that saying "it is rape" gets him out from under the fact that he just called a rape victim a "dope." This is fairly common in evangelical culture—women who go outside the gendered norms and expectations, and then are raped, are "dopes" for not following the prescribed norms that *may* protect them (but are not guaranteed to). The underlying message

*** Full disclosure: the blog post in question was written in response to a friend of mine, blogger Sarah N. Moon.

from Wilson and various other evangelicals? If you simply *behaved* as a woman should, rape wouldn't *happen*.

When you're taught that a woman must behave in a certain way to "deserve" your respect, it is not a hard leap to distrusting her word. And if you cannot trust a woman's word because you don't respect her, how will you not see her as complicit in her own rape, her own assault? If a woman dresses in a way that lowers your respect of her, it's awfully hard to respect that same woman when she becomes a victim. We know these arguments well—"Well, what was she thinking wearing that top/wearing that skirt in that neighborhood/flaunting her body?"

The Threat of Female Sexual Agency

Part of the reason for the lack of discussion in the church surrounding the importance of consent is that acknowledging consent means acknowledging female sexual agency. If a woman can choose to have sex, she just might do it. And she might decide that she is ready before she gets married. And, even worse! she might discover that sex one actively chooses is less likely to be psychologically damaging, which means she might begin to question that whole idea of purity. And then the narrative of shame falls apart.

It's probably not a conscious decision, but rather simply the unquestioned continuance of a narrative. Evangelicals have been repeating this narrative for so long that they don't bother to sit back and wonder if the stories they tell actually involve consent, are actually true examples of the circumstances in which premarital sex might occur. Because all premarital sex must be bad, the American evangelical church has failed to equip its congregants with the ability to tell the difference between sex and rape.

And instead of being taught to identify healthy, consensual sexuality even within marriage, women are taught that it is their marital duty to please their husbands, that sex is supposed to hurt occasionally, and that submission means agreeing to sex even if you don't feel like it. 1 Corinthians 7 (ESV) reads, "For the wife does not have authority over her own body, but the husband does. Likewise the husband does not have authority over his own body, but the wife does." President of the Southern Baptist Theological Seminary Albert Mohler writes, in light of this verse, "At the same time, the husband and wife are ordered to fulfill their marital duties to each other, and not to refrain from sexual union."[50] Denying sex is seen in many Christian circles as denying the gift God has given to a husband and wife.

In this way, evangelicalism seems to have encoded rape into its very theology, casting sex as a duty, no matter what one's mood is at the time. It gives people free rein to rape their spouses, because, after all, one's body is not one's own. If any and all sex before the wedding is a sin, regardless of consent, and all sex after the wedding is a duty, then individual desire, sex drive, and consent are erased in the name of God.

Rape and Sexual Abuse in the Church: Sovereign Grace Ministries

It's important to examine how these narratives of rape and abuse play out in the real world. Sovereign Grace Ministries (SGM) is a large ministry of churches that once included the church Joshua Harris pastors. A current lawsuit alleges that the church, upon learning of various allegations of child sexual abuse, failed in its duty of reporting the cases to the police in a timely manner, and did not even remove the alleged offenders from situations in which they were dealing with children. Several women allege that pastors instructed them that they must submit to their husband's leading, even in cases of sexual and physical abuse. One woman, going by the pseudonym of "Taylor," alleges that pastors told her she "hadn't met her husband's needs physically," when he sexually abused their ten-year-old daughter.[51] Before the court case was dismissed in 2013 due to the statute of limitations, SGM pledged to conduct a "careful review" of the allegations.[52]

T. F. Charlton, a former SGM member and current feminist blogger, wrote in *Salon* about the SGM case:

> It's no accident that so many allegations of serious abuse have arisen across SGM's churches. The combination of patriarchal gender roles, purity culture, and authoritarian clergy that characterizes Sovereign Grace's teachings on parenting, marriage, and sexuality creates an environment where women and children—especially girls—are uniquely vulnerable to abuse.[53]

In response to the case, SGM developed a somewhat terrifying defense—it claimed that the First Amendment protects how the church handles cases of abuse and therefore the secular government did not have the authority to respond or preside over the lawsuit. Specifically, the courts should not have the authority to "second-guess" pastoral care decisions.

You would think that child sexual abuse is something the church could agree is universally bad, and while many, many of the pastors involved would say so, many other pastors connected to SGM either remained entirely silent, pleaded ignorance, or even, in the case of John Piper, vocalized active support for the ministry just weeks after the lawsuit made national news.

We need to commit to pulling our support away from rapists, to showing more sensitivity toward victims of rape, and to believing that when a person says something was not consensual they are not opening themselves up for a debate about it.

We should have a standard of enthusiastic consent—a standard that says nothing but an unequivocal, enthusiastic yes is consent to sex. But because, throughout evangelical culture and into secular culture, we're disinclined to discuss what consent actually is, we've created a world in which rape victims are considered suspect and many victims don't even realize they're victims until it's far too late. Consent is considered by many to be a matter for negotiation, rather than a matter of ownership over one's own body.

Creating a Culture of Consent

It is hard to move away from a culture that allows transgression of boundaries to happen every day, often in small, aggressive ways, into one in which consent is prioritized. But it is possible. There are a few different principles we need to follow to prioritize consent and to create a culture that respects the bodies of others.

1. Respect boundaries

When I was in college, I had a friend, Josh, who had a pretty big personal bubble. He didn't like people being in his space, and he didn't like hugs. So, freshman year, another friend and I took it upon ourselves to sneak-attack him with hugs frequently. Because we'd grown up in a culture that didn't value people's boundaries, we viewed our behavior as perfectly normal. We were "bringing him out of his shell" by forcing physical affection on him.

In reality we drove a wedge in the friendship, and sent the message to Josh that he couldn't trust us. And he was right to distrust us, as we displayed continued disrespect for him. It took years before he and I became truly close as friends—years of learning to *ask* before being physical with him, years of respecting that when he said no to a hug, he really did mean no. Learning to respect his boundaries wasn't just a quirk unique to our relationship, but a necessary education in basic respect for other people's bodies and spaces.

2. Teach others to respect boundaries too

In a related way, we need to teach other people to respect boundaries too. Many of the lessons we learn about consent start very young. I've always been of the mind-set that children are just small adults, which is a surprisingly unusual way to think. They have their own wants, needs, and desires, and are figuring out their personalities and what it means to be a person. This means that when they articulate a need or a feeling, it is important that the adults in their lives listen to and trust them. Teaching children that they will be listened to and that their boundaries will be respected is an important part of building consent culture.

For example, I was once at a Halloween party where I was introduced to a friend's toddler. Being surrounded by a lot of adults in weird costumes, the little boy was scared and hid behind his dad's legs. His father cajoled him to stop hiding and shake my hand. When it became clear that the little boy didn't want to, I lowered my hand and said, "That's OK, Tommy. I can just wave to you from here. It's nice to meet you." Such a gesture conveys understanding of the position a child is in, and tells them that their response is OK, especially when it comes to physical contact.

Teaching our children both to respect the boundaries of others and that their own boundaries will be respected is an important part of a consent culture. And this respect dovetails with the third aspect of creating a consent culture.

3. Believe Survivors

All too often we dehumanize rapists and sexual predators to the point that we imagine them to be monsters lurking in the dark, not our friends, neighbors, brothers, mothers, and colleagues. We exist in a culture of skepticism around rape. It is a very hard thing when a person who has been abused comes forward about their abuse—in a culture of disbelief, they often have nothing to gain and everything to lose, especially if their abuser is someone in a position of power.

But one of the ways we can honor the concept of consent is by believing that people know when their consent has been violated. Instead of asking questions, we can reestablish respect for a person's boundaries by believing that their trauma is real. We shouldn't make debate fodder out of their emotional experience—a move that once again violates important boundaries. We need to become safe people for survivors, people who know and understand consent and can respect them as they reestablish boundaries after a violation.

4. Look out for others

One of the most important parts of a consent culture is community. If we are looking out for our friends' boundaries as well as our own, we create an automatic support group. One of the major complicating factors in a lot of rape and sexual assault cases is the use of drugs and alcohol. A major trope in popular culture is that of getting a woman drunk enough that she wants to have sex—a move that is a violation of consent. If someone doesn't want sex with you sober, they don't want it when they're blackout drunk either.

Unfortunately, this correlation between alcohol and rape results mainly in women being told not to drink to excess. This is a poor solution to the problem, as it simply moves the rapist's attention to a different woman. A much better solution is to have an ethic wherein you look out for the well-being of others. See a girl trying to pressure a guy into drinks at the bar when he's clearly not into it? Step in and make it clear that it's not OK. A guy you don't know is trying to give your visibly drunk friend a ride home? Stick around and make sure you both get home safe.

Step in for your friends. Say something—be that person who is willing to risk some embarrassment to protect their friends. By turning consent into a communal ethic, a standard by which *everyone* needs to operate, we can make great strides toward developing a healthy culture of consent.

Consent is something we cannot take lightly. We must approach it with seriousness, in every situation, checking in with our partners, with our spouses, with our friends. We need to respect the people around us, regardless of what they're wearing and regardless of whether they turn us on. Respect is key to a healthy sexual ethic. It makes us better as people, and better as lovers.

CHAPTER TWELVE

Only You Can Define Your Sexuality

When I was a kid, my parents cut most of my hair off because I refused to let them brush it. I distinctly remember, when I was four or five, actually crawling inside my clothes hamper and hiding to avoid the terror of the brush. I didn't want to pull my hair back; I didn't want it to look "nice." It hurt when my hair was brushed because it would get so tangled from playing outside that cutting it off was preferable.

I also was the girl who always had male friends. My best friend when I was in second grade was a small blond boy named Phillip whose backyard was diagonal to my own. I did everything with Phil. My family had a pool, so in the summer he'd come over and we'd spend hours swimming together. We had a fort under the deck in the backyard. In the winter we'd pile snow up under his deck and jump from the second story into the pile—it's remarkable that I made it through my youth without a broken bone. He was my best friend.

Until I switched to his school. Open enrollment ended in my district, which meant I could no longer go to the school where my dad was principal and instead had to switch to the elementary school within walking distance. Suddenly my friendships with guys and my tomboy behavior were cause for concern. Boys teased me about "like-liking" my guy friends. Girls teased me about acting like a boy. At eight years old, I felt extreme pressure to fit in. It was during this time that I also learned the words *bitch* and *faggot*.

The socialization of gender is insidious. I, as a cisgender woman, still received teasing and maltreatment because I played with gender roles as a child, refusing to be the little girl made of sugar and spice and everything nice. I was in detention more often than I was at sleepovers and it wasn't until middle school that I began to be accepted by girls enough to have girl friends. Improper gender performance by a small child scared people.

In evangelicalism, gender and sexuality are fused in an unbreakable bond. How well one behaves in accordance to their gendered roles is an indicator of whom one is attracted to, and vice versa, and this affects everyone—straight and queer—though not in the same ways. So if you have a boy who likes to pretend-cook and use My Little Pony toothpaste? Don't be surprised if he faces derision in the grocery store and comments implying that he might turn out to be "one of those."

And little girls who love to climb trees, hate wearing lace, and cut their hair short?

Welcome to my life.

This is where the development of a personal sexual ethic can become controversial. Vital to personal ethics is the knowledge that gender and sexuality are not fixed states. Rather they are fluid, intermingling identities, and a healthy sexual ethic does not demand that a person change how they identify in order to practice it. In other words, a sexual ethic that applies only to straight people who have never questioned their gender? Is no ethic at all.

Whom you love, and how you perform your gender, are deeply, deeply personal, and are things only *you* can decide. Taking room for yourself to suss all of it out is vitally important to a healthy understanding of sexuality.

Gender as a Staged Performance

Much of our sexual ethic in the existing evangelical church is tied to the ways in which we comply with existing rules of gender. What gender looks like, for men and women, changes depending upon a combination of cultural cues and an internal sense of identity.

Gender identity and assigned sex are two separate things. An assigned sex is the designation given at birth based on physical characteristics. Gender identity is an internal sense of what one's gender is. For cisgender people, the sex assigned at birth and the internal gender identity match—a cisgender woman feels like a woman, and her genitals are recognized as female. For trans* people, however, internal gender identity and assigned sex do not match.

Transwomen *are* women, who have sexual characteristics that are read as male. Transmen *are* men, who have sexual characteristics that are read as female. Completing the spectrum, genderqueer and nonbinary trans* people don't readily identify with either part of the binary and instead see themselves existing between the two (in some cultures, they are referred to as "the third gender").

Many trans* people will start hormone therapy and undergo surgery, if these are available to them, in order to make their outer expression match their mental picture of themselves. Many, in the years before they make these physical changes, will live as the gender they feel they best express. Some choose not to transition at all.

Ultimately, there are socially conditioned signals about what it means to be a man or a woman, and we receive these signals through how people react to us as we grow. This is known as the *performance of gender*. How well we perform our gender depends on the social cues we get from the culture surrounding us. For example, in the United States, masculinity is often performed by participation in acts of violence or strength. Feminine performance, in contrast, is often quiet, demure, and dainty.

I've cut my hair short several times over my life, sporting a curly pixie cut each time. Inevitably some stranger calls me "sir" or mistakes me for a young man. This misgendering reinforces that I am not performing femininity well enough to be seen as a woman in my culture.

The evangelical church is one of the entities most heavily engaged in policing the performance of gender—partly because the entire sexual ethic of purity culture is invested in strictly enforced gender roles.

Sexuality Is Fluid and Complex

Like the performance of gender, sexuality occurs on a fluid spectrum. Sexuality is determined only by the person it concerns. As an adult, I've spent a lot of time learning about my own sexuality, something that, oddly enough, sexual experience brought to the forefront. When I was nearly twenty-seven, I realized that I wasn't *just* attracted to men, but also to genderqueer people and women. I've always liked men who perform their gender in more effeminate ways, so it wasn't necessarily a surprise to me to realize that my sexuality encompassed much more than just cisgender men. I realized, in other words, that I am one of the 10 to 14 percent of women in the United States who experience a fluid sexual identity.

Sexual identity is, in its essence, about sexual attraction. Whom we are attracted to has the ability to expand or shift over time. It can also remain completely static, depending on where you fall on the sexuality spectrum. It is up to the person concerned to know themselves well enough to explore their attraction and feelings and figure out where they land on the spectrum of sexuality. No one else can decide that.

This is an immutable fact of living within a community—people are complex, fascinating beings, and to shove them into unwanted boxes is to degrade who God made them to be. We dehumanize people when we deny them access to understanding about themselves. Therefore, I will stand for nothing less than affirmation of all sexual and gender identities as valid.†††

---

††† This affirmation comes with a "consenting adult" caveat. There are existing arguments about pedophilia being a sexual orientation that is just as valid as homosexuality. This is where consent comes into play—it is literally impossible to act upon a pedophiliac desire without causing harm to a person, because by nature children are incapable of consent. Arguments that pedophilia and homosexuality are merely two different orientations on the same spectrum neglect consent as a necessary determining factor.

We have a tendency to box and label certain identities as "broken" and "in need of redemption." Trans* and LGB folks are currently popular targets for such attempts, though it is growing more and more unpopular to proclaim that LGBT-ness is something that needs "fixing." But beyond that, evangelicalism instills a "fix-it" attitude into theories about marriage, about sex lives, about everything involving sexual identity. We need to remove ourselves from this mindset—people are not things to be fixed.

Similarly, we must remember that sexuality is fluid. A person's sexuality can change over time and giving people the freedom to explore and understand themselves (as long as they are not hurting others in the process) is important. Many of the women I interviewed explained to me that they didn't realize their bisexuality or asexuality until after they were involved in a heterosexual marriage. This doesn't mean that they ran out and started having sex with women, but that they did some private reassessment of who they were in the context of a straight relationship. We need, first and foremost, to honor other people's stories and other people's identities. In evangelical-speak, this is meeting people where they are. But I would add the following caveat: we must meet people where they are without a desire to change them into our image of what they should be.

Instead of meeting people where they are, however, purity culture makes two false assumptions about its audience. First, that everyone is cisgender, identifying with the gender that matches their birth designation, and second, that everyone is heterosexual. This creates confusion, pain, and depression for people who do not fit the binary category of "cis man who likes women" or "cis woman who likes men."

Language as Violence

Much of the language and theology espoused by the evangelical church relies on a strict view of gender identity. Even the metaphors the church uses to talk about God rely on a conception of marriage as an exclusively heterosexual, cisgender institution. This kind of marriage is often used as an analogy for the relationship between Christ and the Church—the church is the (female) Bride of Christ, and Christ is the loving husband. Everything within these metaphors and ideas is coded in terms of binary gender and heterosexuality. This language erases the identities of the very people sitting in the pews of churches of America every Sunday.

The language preached from the pulpit often does violence to trans* individuals. Mark Driscoll is one of the worst offenders, with sermons on what it means to be a "manly man" and reinforcing strict ideas about what women and men are "like." For example, in the summer of 2011, Mark Driscoll posted a Facebook status making fun of "effeminate" worship pastors, indicating that such people make him feel uncomfortable.[54] He often speaks of masculinity and femininity in rigid, unyielding terms, tying masculinity specifically to strength and violence (his fanatic love of mixed martial arts is legendary) and tying "womanhood" to quiet servitude and graciousness.

Throughout purity culture, it is an accepted fact that homosexuality and variant gender identities are sins. But such an assumption dehumanizes the very people God has created and makes judgments that are not ours to make. A personal sexual ethic needs to be one that allows other people to live out their gender and their sexuality as they see fit, so long as it doesn't involve hurting other people. The church, through the twentieth and twenty-first centuries, has spent far too much time emphasizing the judgment of sin for LGBT people and not nearly enough time engaging in loving community with them. A healthy view of gender and sexuality needs to account for all people as image-bearers of the Divine. We need to take care to reflect this in our language.

Virginity as a Social Construct, a Process, Not an Event

Those who do not identify on the gender binary are not the only ones hurt by purity and gender narratives within the church. Gay and bisexual youth also find themselves unable to connect with these narratives. After all, how does a woman save herself for her future husband if she's a lesbian? How do you "lose" your virginity as a gay cis man if virginity is defined as a penis entering a vagina? Does a bisexual person lose their virginity twice?

Purity movements are *necessarily* dependent on heterosexuality. Such dependence automatically excludes people who are not straight—people God created. The image of virginity, in itself, is constructed around heterosexual intercourse. Virginity, in the purity movement, consists of a penis entering a vagina—nothing more, nothing less. As a result, virginity is a limited social construct that cannot be universally applied, despite the church's attempts. Calls to save one's virginity for marriage are useless to people for whom virginity loss is ambiguous at best.

It is important, then, that our discussions of virginity and purity apply to those for whom the distinctions are not clear bright lines. We must honor the idea that sexuality is fluid and that virginity is not simply one thing or one act.

Rather than the loss of virginity being a singular act defined by a penis entering a vagina, we should look at virginity loss as a process. For many, virginity loss may occur when penis-in-vagina intercourse happens. For some it will be another, different event—the first time they perform or receive oral sex, for example, or maybe the first time they're naked with someone. Because it is so nebulous, what constitutes virginity ends up being a personal decision. Only you can decide when you've "lost" your virginity, according to your own personal experience. Our language is currently inadequate to address this issue—we don't even have a word in English for someone who is not a virgin, despite "non-virgin" being the state most people are in.

Virginity exists as a state of being. There is no one event that can remove a person's virginity. There is no singular moment when you shift from being a virgin to not being one. It is a process that happens over time, as you experience more sexually and as you grow and know yourself well enough to develop an idea of what sex means to you.

This discussion of virginity-as-process is actually a baptizing of a purity movement concept—that of emotional purity. Somewhere along the line, severely conservative evangelicals and fundamentalists realized that "saving one's virginity" was an inadequate concept (though it is still dominant in many areas). "Emotional purity" was then invented. It is centered on the idea that one can lose purity by becoming emotionally involved, even if physical experience doesn't happen.

Emotional purity, however, is a concept still tainted by a misogynist heteronormativity (it is almost always discussed in terms of female emotional attachment, rarely male). It is not part of an effort to include LGBT people in the conversation on holiness and purity but rather another means of reinforcing control of cis-hetero women's bodies.

When we turn virginity into a process, we move it out of the physical realm and into the emotional one. When virginity is moved from event to feeling, we risk entering the realm of "emotional purity." To be clear, virginity-as-process is not about emotional purity. It is a redefining of both concepts. Process virginity allows individuals to make the decisions that are right for them, to understand and know their own feelings about their bodies and their experiences. It puts bodily autonomy back into the hands of those who own the bodies, whether they be cis, trans*, genderqueer, straight, gay, poly, or bi. By beginning with the idea that the definitions of virginity loss and sex are up to the individual, we develop an ethic that recognizes the personal nature of sexuality and gender identity, and removes bodies from comment in the public sphere.

Safe Spaces, People, and the Church

When developing these ethics, we need to take care that we create safe spaces within the church for people to feel comfortable with their identities. Whether or not someone is "safe" for another person is a feminist value that often gets ignored and outright reviled within the church. Yet for non-binary, non-heterosexual folk, safety is of the utmost importance. A safe person is someone marginalized people can trust to treat them as human beings, not as projects to be fixed.

One idea popular throughout evangelical culture comes from Oxford professor and children's author C. S. Lewis. In his popular series *The Chronicles of Narnia*, the Jesus figure, Aslan, appears to Narnians as a great majestic lion. At one point in the books, one character, Mr. Beaver, is telling Lucy Pevensie about Aslan. Lucy asks if Aslan is safe, and Mr. Beaver replies, "Who said anything about safe?...'Course he isn't safe. But he's good. He's the King, I tell you."[55]

Many evangelicals have latched on to this image of God, embracing God as an unsafe but good being. We cannot *tame* God, so why should we care about safety? Unfortunately, such a conception of God reads as hogwash to those people whose very existence is wrapped up in whether or not people in their lives are *safe*.

LGB individuals are four times more likely to commit suicide than any other group—excepting trans* individuals, who are twelve times more likely.[56]

LGBT youth are more likely to be homeless—often as a result of being rejected from their homes and cut off from family. As a result, LGBT youth are also much more likely to be the victims of violent crimes, more likely to be discriminated against in the job market, and more likely to have unstable and unsafe living situations. They are looking for safe spaces and safe people, and unfortunately, in many areas, these are few and far between.

As a church, we participate in this violence when we allow LGBT identities to be a debatable issue, when we hold up a person's safety and personhood as matters of theological debate. By clinging to its gender essentialism, to the idea that *man* and *woman* are defined, immutable categories and labels, the church participates in the oppression of the most vulnerable persons in our society. With our cavalier discussion of gendered issues, we erase and oppress whole swaths of people, rather than helping to alleviate the burden of their oppression, rather than seeing them as fully human and implementing what Jesus said was the second-greatest commandment: "Love your neighbor as yourself."

Safety may seem like a small thing, but it really truly makes a difference when you have grown up in an environment where your very existence is denied in every sermon about sexual activity and you are told that your very being is somehow broken, wrong, and sinful. Safety is a vital part of goodness, and we must work on being safe people for others—and safe people for ourselves.

What This All Means for Your Personal Sexual Ethics

No one can determine your sexuality or gender identity but you. How you choose to perform your gender and whom you choose to love are matters of such a deeply personal nature that it is impossible for anyone else to understand them as well as you do. Determining who you are is a long—often a lifetime—process, so don't be afraid of the questions, of the struggle, of the discomfort. Learning to be yourself is a vital part of developing a healthy sexuality, so do your level best not to suppress those feelings and ideas, even if they're a little bit scary.

Give yourself the room and the respect to understand yourself. You're a human, you're created and loved by God.

Now get to know what that means for you. Explore your identities; ask yourself the scary questions. All too often, we are the first people to deny our identities—it took me twenty-six years to figure out mine, and I'm still exploring. That means you can too. If we allow ourselves the room to question, to recognize that sexualities and means of gender expression outside the heterosexual gender binary are normal, natural, and OK, we will help create an environment that is safe for all people, not just those who fit society's norms. We will create a new normal.

Gaining comfort in your identity is a hard thing to do, especially if it's an identity that places you in a marginalized group. But it is ultimately a journey that will put you at peace with who you are—and the healthiest sexual ethics extend from people who are at peace with themselves. Whoever you are, you are loved by a God who finds you beautiful and wants you to be fulfilled in life. Be a safe space for yourself first; then you can learn to be a safe space for others.

CHAPTER THIRTEEN

Sex Without Shame

The car rolled down the highway, eating up the miles between home and us. The sun was setting behind us, and it was quiet on the prairie. My mother and I had gone out of town for the day to visit family and were on our way back. I was excitedly telling her about my writing projects and babbling on about gender identities and issues facing the LGBT population when her silence made me pause. I could tell a question was waiting.

"Dianna, are you gay?"

I hesitated for a moment before answering, and I could feel my mom's breath catching. She was in her sixties, had never lived outside South Dakota, and had been taught all her life that homosexuality is a sin. The possibility that I could be *one of those* scared her.

"Well. No. But I am kind of bi? I mean, I mostly am attracted to men, but if the right woman came along, I wouldn't turn it down."

She paused for a minute, taking in the information,

and then asked what, to her, was a logical follow-up: "Have you had sex?"

This was the big moment. The moment when she learned what she'd kind of always suspected—that her daughter, her only daughter, wasn't going to be a virgin on her wedding day, wasn't "worthy" of the purity ring she'd worn.

"I have. It was…fun. I don't regret it at all."

I braced myself for the lecture, but she didn't even seem disappointed.

"You consented and everything? You wanted to?"

"Yes, absolutely, it was my idea!"

"How do you feel about it?"

"Ehhhh, I don't regret the act, but I do wish I'd had a different attitude going into it."

"OK. I understand that."

And that was how I came out to my mother. The "confession" strengthened our relationship, made us closer as mother and daughter, and made it possible for us to discuss things in our lives more openly and with more grace. She didn't approach the topic with shame or disappointment or even any kind of judgment, allowing me to feel comfortable and loved and safe.

Unfortunately, for so many of the people I've spoken to over the last year and a half of researching this project, such a story would be an anomaly. Many, when talking about their sexual experiences (through consensual acts or assault), have found themselves walled off from their community, pushed away from any help or any kind of grace. The shame we heap upon women happens in denominations all across the country, compounding and creating hurt.

And all this in the name of Christ.

The Toxicity of Shame

If you take one lesson and one lesson only from this book, I want it to be this: God doesn't function in a currency of shame. Shame isn't from God, it isn't of God, and it isn't something Christians should engage in. Shame is not nor will it ever be a useful response to a person's experience of the world, especially when it comes to sexual experiences.

Whatever you have done, whatever has happened to you, whatever people have told you: shame is not the answer. You are worthy of love, you are worthy of grace, and you have no reason to be ashamed.

Shame is a toxic substance that the modern evangelical church is really comfortable with—because shaming and judging others is a human response. If people don't fit the white, able-bodied, heterosexual, cisgender model, it's very easy for us to respond in ways that shame them for being different. As communal creatures, we tend to commune with those who are Just Like Us, and anything Other is cause for concern.

But this toxic shame doesn't reflect a gracious forgiveness or even a compassionate understanding of another person. It sees a person as an Other—something separate from humanity. Shame tries to force them back into line by ostracizing them and telling them they are bad people. I'll never forget a trend when I was a senior in high school, to walk past a girl who was rumored to have had sex and sing, "Ess Tee Dee" in a low voice. And we felt justified in doing it because that person was not a person to us—she was wholly Other and had failed to live up to standards we had for our own lives.

We knew nothing of those girls as people. As a result, we allowed shame to reign supreme. And that is neither godly nor Christlike.

Recovering from Shame: Toward a New Sexual Ethic

So how do we step away from this? How do we prevent shame from being the common currency with which we discuss sex? How do we begin to implement these principles?

Our motto in approaching sexual ethics needs to be that of doctors: "First, do no harm." When we meet people where they are, we do so with the goal of seeing them as people, of understanding them as people, and of affirming their story and their journey. We have our own journey and our own difficulties to deal with, and attempting to control or decide for another person what their sexual ethics should be can cause much more harm than good. We need to approach the issue with the utmost care and grace and love and mercy, not rules and legalistic screeds about Deuteronomy 22.

In addition to doing no harm with our rhetoric, we need to make sure our personal sexual behaviors do not harm others. This is of utmost importance to the community that surrounds us. This lens honors a Biblical sexual ethic: do not sin by bringing harm to your neighbor. In John 13 (NIV), Jesus asks that we "love one another. As I have loved you, so you must love one another." We must treat others with respect and care and love.

The Apostle Paul says in 1 Corinthians (NIV), "'I have the right to do anything,' you say—but not everything is beneficial. 'I have the right to do anything'—but not everything is constructive. No one should seek their own good, but the good of others." A sexual ethic should start here—in seeking the good of others. We need to take care, in our personal journeys through sexuality, not to harm or cause problems for other people. We need to sensitively live within community while simultaneously being true to ourselves.

Paul emphasized a lot of community work, as the way the early church functioned and grew was dependent upon the grace and mercy of a community working out its issues together, with a mind toward grace and love for all its members. We see Paul, again and again, smacking down people who would attempt to use the community for their own gain or to use other people for their own ends. We need to develop a sexual ethic that does not depend on using other people for our own manipulation and pleasure. We should not objectify people in our quest to understand ourselves.

This is a Christian sexual ethic fundamentally better than purity theology. In not using other people, we honor their humanity, we honor God-in-Them, and we ensure that the give-and-take of sexual acts is happening with healthy boundaries and healthy attitudes. Note that this doesn't necessarily mean marriage—because marriage is not necessarily the best environment for healthy sexuality, at least not by default. People's motivations and conceptions of their own selves matter, as does the context of the relationship. The marriage bed is not automatically clean, and the non-marriage bed is not automatically defiling. What matters is the way in which we honor other people.

In this sense, there exists a sexual ethic that applies to married and unmarried alike, regardless of where a person falls on the spectrum of experience or orientation. As

Christians, we need to honor other people by not using them as objects to our own ends. This means that a married sexual relationship in which a wife is using her husband as a human vibrator and an unmarried one in which a guy is using his partner to get his rocks off are equally unhealthy and equally sinful. Christian sexual ethics need to be about honoring the humanity of individuals, and honoring the community in which we live and breathe. This is not a matter of *when* sex happens, but rather a matter of attitudes, postures, and understanding.

Whether it is your first or your thousandth time, sex needs to be approached with respect for the humanity of everyone involved.

Mutual Pleasure and Mutual Consent: Taking Shame out of the Equation

Part of honoring other people means that a healthy sexual relationship is one based in mutual pleasure and mutual enthusiastic consent. This is absolute and fundamental. Rape has no part in healthy sexual ethics. Sexual assault has no place in healthy sexual ethics. All partners involved must be consenting and gaining pleasure from the encounter. This requires attentiveness on the part of both partners, communication about what feels good and what does not, and an understanding that the activity stops the instant one or the other feels uncomfortable with what is happening. This is baseline sexual ethics, and it extends from loving and appreciating one's partner as a complex person created by God who deserves to be loved as we love ourselves.

Sexuality is a many-splendored thing, and has the capacity to be life-affirming and life-giving. But it must be approached from a position where we recognize other people as people, not just objects that could provide plea-sure. And how we handle our sexuality in private needs to be extended into how we discuss sexuality within the church. For too long we have discussed sexuality in terms of shame. We have talked about regret, about pain, about how premarital sex kills, about how women who hook up are less-than, not fully people.

This needs to come to end. God does not function within a currency of shame. God is not the angry God of Jonathan Edwards, dangling us like spiders over a fiery pit. That image of God pushes people away from life-giving community, away from the grace and beauty and mercy that are a loving, merciful, communal relationship with other humans. By injecting shame, especially into something as personal as sexuality, we turn words of grace and freedom into blunt objects for beating people into submission. We buy into sinful patriarchal structures that say that men and women are genders first and people second. We buy into harmful rape cultures that blame victims for their own rapes. We treat women as public property, open for comment and use. We create a church unable to commu-nicate with the outside world, one that sets itself further and further away from actual people and becomes a bastion of shame and guilt for so many.

Evangelicalism in America needs to fundamentally change the way it approaches sexual ethics. We need to inject grace and remove shame. We need to stop telling women that they are damaged goods and instead encourage healthy sexual relationships and understanding of other people. We need to meet people where they are, and it is impossible to do that when we are setting up a wall of shame and a list of rules. We need to reject the patriarchy, as Jesus did. We need to reject a world of concrete traditional gender roles. There is no room in God's new world for shoving people into boxes and shaming them into place. There is no place for harming others in the name of holiness. And there is no place for shame here.

Your Feelings Are Valid: It's OK to Be Who You Are

One peculiar part of evangelical culture is the all-too-frequent pushback against strong emotions—anger in many circles is considered a sin. When I first started exploring my sexuality and discovering that my church upbringing had actually stunted my understanding of it, I was angry. But having grown up in a world where distrusting your emotions—especially in reaction to Christian teachings—was the norm, it was very hard for me to accept that anger, to understand that it was healthy, and to heal from it.

In my conversations with women at different stages in their faith journeys, one thing many of them observed was that they had been encouraged to ignore their own discomfort, their own conscience regarding issues of women's sexual roles and purity. Many of them sensed that something was wrong, but couldn't place it, couldn't pin it down, and were encouraged to try to make their feelings fit in with God's Word—in other words, ignore it and it'll go away.

But that's the thing about feelings of uncertainty and

doubt—shoving them down doesn't make them go away. Shaming yourself for having them doesn't make them go away. And while spending time in God's Word can be useful, dealing with your own feelings and reactions is vitally important for figuring out how things apply to your own life.

One of the questions you may have is how you sort out what you like and don't like, what you need and what it means to be ready. How do you reach a comfortable emotional place where you can have a reaction and not immediately want to sublimate it into some mold of what a woman should be? You need to allow yourself to feel.

Ask yourself—what is making me feel this way? What, actually, is this emotion? After a lifetime of being told to listen to God instead of your heart, it's very hard to switch over to using your feelings as a guiding mechanism. But it is vitally important that you begin this process of understanding and dealing with yourself and your gut reactions and your emotions, because it is step one in learning how to rid yourself of shame.

You have been told that listening to your gut reactions means that you're not listening to the Holy Spirit. But I'd like propose a radical idea: maybe that gut reaction *is* the still small voice of the Spirit. God is a God of peace and love and grace and mercy, yes—but God is also a God who feels your hurt and your pain and your anger, and God is angry at injustices just as you are angry. Contrary to popular evangelical belief, feeling anger is not a sin—you're allowed to feel angry. You should feel angry. Being outraged at mistreatment is normal and even good.

How you respond to your anger is vital as well—you don't have to be nice about it. The worst myth Christians are told today is that "niceness" is how we set ourselves apart from a sinful world. "Niceness" covers a multitude of sins. But if you are angry, allow yourself to be angry. Allow yourself to express that anger—allow yourself to experience it, express it, and then let it go, if that's what you need. Not immediately, not all at once. Sometimes it takes years to learn to understand and express anger at how the church has been complicit in injustice. I've still not fully let go of my anger—and I hope I never get rid of all of it.

Anger bubbles up when you realize that you've not been equipped well for sex—that you are forever playing catch-up in your sexual education. But we need to be careful not to swing in the opposite direction and shame those who are not experienced. One problem that many Christians find with sex-positive feminism is that it seems to be encouraging a wanton world of anything-goes sexuality and hookups every weekend. Virgins often feel shamed by this culture. I remember being saddened and horrified to learn that only 4 percent of people in my generation reach their twenty-fifth birthday as a virgin. The disappointment I felt upon learning this was hard to deal with—I felt like I was missing out on an adult experience, like I was broken in some way. It took me a while to recognize that this disappointment was an extension of shame over not being what I thought other people wanted me to be. I felt like a freak because I was a feminist, a Christian, and a virgin. I had to realize the source of my shame, and then let it go.

Shame based on sexual status, whether it is because of lots of sexual activity or none at all, is wrong. All of it. I want to affirm as strongly as I can—virginity is not the problem here. Virginity is not something to be ashamed of, nor is it an emblem of prudishness. There are people for whom waiting until marriage is the absolute right choice for their personal lives and their journeys. That is OK.

The problem comes when we assign moral value to that virginity or non-virginity, from either end. How we talk about our experience is a moral choice. We need to first and foremost remove the moral judgment from the discussion, and one of the ways we do that is by saying it's OK to be a virgin. And it's OK not to be a virgin. Your story, your life, is more important than whether or not you've "lost it."

You Are Whole: Getting Rid of Shame by Talking About Sex

So how do we honor personal journeys? Drop the analogies. The only thing that a sexually active person is? Is a person. Full stop. You are not used-up rags, you are not goods returned as damaged, you are not a torn-up rose or a chewed-up Oreo cookie. You are not damaged beyond repair. Regardless of your sexual state, you are a human being, you are a created person of God, and you are whole.

Instead of talking about waiting for marriage, we need to talk about waiting until we're ready. Instead of shaming sexually active young people, we need to be equipping them with the knowledge to have sex safely. Instead of categorizing all premarital sexual activity as bad, we need to have conversations about consent, and pleasure, and peer pressure.

What does readiness look like? It means being comfortable enough with yourself and your partner to enthusiastically consent. It is not determined by age, but rather by a mature mental state. Some people reach this state at sixteen, some not until they're thirty-five. Readiness is ultimately your decision. But there are some guideposts along the way—do you know yourself well enough to know this is what you want? Ask yourself *why* you are doing something. Rather than just telling yourself no because "the Bible says," interrogate your ideas. Do you want to do something because *you* want to do it? Or because you feel like you *should*?

Other questions you can ask to determine readiness are: "Am I doing this because I feel like I'm the last virgin on earth and I need to 'get it over with,' or am I doing it because I feel it is the right thing for me?" "Am I prepared to have this encounter safely—do I have access to birth control and condoms?" "Do I trust my partner well enough to know that they will stop if I ask them to stop? Do I feel comfortable telling them no?" And "What do I hope to gain from this encounter?"

These are hard questions that can help guide young adults toward understanding themselves and their readiness level when it comes to pursuing a sexual relationship. We also need to talk about what a sexual encounter should feel like. And in doing so, we affirm that the decision to wait and the decision not to wait are both valid choices. If you are not ready, we must respect that as an individual choice for your life—no one should be made to feel pressure or shame because of the "status" of their genitals, and that includes people who are waiting for their wedding night.

But we need to *talk* about it—about what those choices mean to each of us, what it means for us to feel ready, and why we're waiting. And no, "God said so and therefore everyone should wait" doesn't count as talking.

Setting Boundaries: How We Talk About Sex

But what does talking about it look like, practically? The discussion is different for everyone, but there are a few things we can keep in mind.

First, we need to teach children the proper terms and concepts about their bodies. Instead of using silly euphemisms that distance us from our bodies, we need to use the correct terms—it's not a "muffin"; it's a vulva and a vagina. It's not a "wiener"; it's a penis. These lessons help us to become comfortable with our body parts, and help children to identify with their own bodies and be comfortable in them from an early age. And while I almost hate to mention it, it helps to have an established vocabulary so that if the way a child talks about their body suddenly changes, a parent can know that a form of abuse might be going on.

Second, we need to respect the boundaries of other people. When someone sets a boundary, we need to respect and honor it—especially if it is around their body.

And third, we need to practice having these discussions. Create safe environments where having discussions about sex and sexual boundaries and sexual readiness is welcome. These spaces need to be free of judgment, free of persecution, and free of fear. The only way we do this is by learning how to be safe people and committing ourselves to an ethic of love instead of shame. We must listen. We must empathize. We must respect people's right to be closeted. We must respect that the stories people tell us are told in confidence, unless those people have given us permission to share. We must ask for permission before we pray for someone. We must ask what they need, not what we can do. This is safety. This is how we have these important conversations.

Conversations About Pleasure, Not Shame

When we talk about sexuality, we also have conversations about pleasure. These are scary conversations. Not many parents want to talk with their young teenage daughters about how sex is supposed to *feel*, and that's understandable—but a conversation about making sure that sex feels good and that you have the right to stop things if it stops feeling good is massively important for preparing people to understand their own sexual encounters. Understanding that sex is supposed to be pleasurable and consensual can empower people to communicate more with their partners and to understand what they want. This baseline has helped me communicate with my own partners and create healthy connections that deepen relationships.

So we must talk about readiness. We must talk about consent. We must talk about pleasure. We must talk openly about sex without making false promises about what sex after marriage is supposed to look like. In doing these things, we change our sexual ethic from a simple, universal no to a more complex understanding of healthy sexuality that helps us to know ourselves, to know our partners, and to understand where our sexual activity fits within the spectrum of our lives. For some, understanding their own sexual ethic will mean waiting until marriage. For others, it will mean having a mutually pleasurable and consensual encounter on a first date.

In a healthy world, sexuality will be divorced from shame and sin and darkness, and be brought into the light, placed in its proper spot in our lives. Staying a virgin until marriage will no longer be a point of pride, but merely another state of being. In expanding sexuality into a more universal ethic that allows each person to determine their readiness and their interpretations of what that means, we create a world in which sexuality is not shameful or scary, but just another everyday part of becoming the person God made us to be. And that is the all-important point.

Loving Thy Neighbor

Now let's circle back around to the most important commandment of all: loving one's neighbor. In these discussions and in these life experiences, grace rather than shame needs to be the rule of the day. This is how we live out a Christian life and move into a healthy sexuality—we love our neighbor as we love ourselves; we create a world in which our neighbor can speak openly and fearlessly about their life and their experiences without being haunted by the shame of "not doing it right" or "not being enough."

Loving our neighbor means dropping our judgments at the door. It means taking people's whole lives into account. And it means learning to love through grace and mercy, not through shame masked as truth-telling.

This is the only way out of the darkness. This is the only way to save our children. We must let them be the men and women they are, even if it doesn't align with our hopes for them.

We aren't the children of a God of shame. We aren't subjected to a God of wrath, nor are we sinners in the hands of an angry God. We are part of the new inheritance, children of God—a God who does not shame, whose Holy Spirit is with us to guide us in her ways, and who approaches each individual life in the way that individual life needs. No two children of God are the same, which means no two children of God will approach sexual experience in exactly the same way.

But in loving our neighbors, in treating others as the children of God they are, we can help to create the shame-free community of God here on earth. We can love in grace and mercy and leave sinful shame behind us. We can live.

Epilogue

When I finished my first semester of teaching at Baylor University—a semester that included the ups and downs of trying to figure out how to teach and teach well—I spent the last day of class giving the students a benediction of sorts. I read aloud my favorite poem—Alfred, Lord Tennyson's "Ulysses." The poem functions as a kind of nineteenth-century fanfiction—Ulysses, the main character from Homer's *Iliad* and *Odyssey*, is an old man, going out on one last adventure, passing reign over his kingdom to his son, Telemachus. Tennyson's take is inspiring, a vision of a world infinitely changeable and forever changed by our presence in it. In the last lines, Ulysses (the poem's speaker), says:

> *Death closes all: but something ere the end,*
> *Some work of noble note, may yet be done,*
> *Not unbecoming men that strove with Gods.*
> *The lights begin to twinkle from the rocks:*
> *The long day wanes: the slow moon climbs: the deep*
> *Moans round with many voices. Come, my friends,*
> *'Tis not too late to seek a newer world.*
>
> ...

DAMAGED GOODS

We are not now that strength which in old days
Moved earth and heaven; that which we are, we are;
One equal temper of heroic hearts,
Made weak by time and fate, but strong in will
To strive, to seek, to find, and not to yield.

I chose this poem because I believe—as a progressive, as a woman, as a Christian—that we must always fight the hard fights, we must push forward, "to strive, to seek, to find, and not to yield." Tennyson's character is talking about great Greek adventurers, but the beauty of looking forward, of striving, of performing noble works with our lives, is a pull we all feel. And it is this message that I wish to leave the women in the church.

When I was still a conservative Christian, I thought I might be called to minister to single people within the church, to let them know they had worth in spite of the "must get married/ring by spring/race to the altar" culture that surrounded them. Even then I knew worth was something that lay outside of one's marital state, in spite of an upbringing that told me otherwise, that told me to expect a husband in or shortly after college; in spite of a church that told me I could be good at ministry (but never a pastor) while I "waited" for my husband to come by.

If you find yourself failing under the weight and expectation of the shaming that declares a person's moral state lands somewhere in their nether regions, I hope you will remember you are worth something. I hope too that you will find a way to articulate your discomfort with patriarchal norms, to press for a better, holier, holistic understanding of sexuality and abstinence and sexual activity. And it is my sincerest hope that you will find a way toward understanding yourself, toward making good decisions with your life (whatever those decisions may be) and toward articulate communication about who *you* are as an individual, created and loved by God. No, this isn't an altar call.

I have one last principle to impart to you, and that's a principle I've learned to live my life by. It is twofold. First, we must always be questioning. Question everything—question yourself, question your church leaders, question me. It is freeing to know that you no longer have to be afraid of the hard questions and where they might lead. It is not a sin to strive with God—indeed, it is a basic part of what makes us human.

The second part is this: doubt is OK. I faced a lot of pushback when I started to doubt the American church's narratives about purity and sexuality. It created a lot of fights and rifts. It was a struggle—I was one of the first people in my circle of blogging to actively question the merit of our focus on virginity. It was a long, lonely time, during which I faced verbal attacks from family members for challenging their narratives, during which setting boundaries became a necessary, important part of my emotional health. But allowing my doubt to sneak into my life helped me to understand myself as an individual and where my relationships and my relationship to God stood. Had I clung to the idea that doubt is illegitimate, that doubting teachings on sexuality in the church necessarily meant doubting my faith as a whole, I might have ended up in a place I didn't want to be—trapped within a patriarchal box of sin and shame, calling myself damaged goods and allowing my need for a black-and-white answer to dictate everything I did.

Instead I challenge you to embrace the messiness, to

walk away from the black and white, and to see people, not sluts and virgins, not horny guys and demure girls, not married folks and damaged goods. Let doubt creep into your narrative, let people be people, and let your eyes be opened to a new, messy, lovely community of people who are both whole and broken in paradoxical, wonderful ways. Certainty is the enemy of faith, and doubt and questioning are necessary companions on our journeys through the sacred and profane realm that is human life.

Last, I want you to remember that you are loved. In your fullness, in your brokenness, in your inconsistencies, in your high highs and low lows, you are worthy of love because you are a human being and that means you have worth. You have worth because you are *you*. No one else can be you or occupy your selfsame space within the universe. This is what grace is—understanding that you, in all your contradictions and heresies and mistakes and achievements, have something to contribute to this vast thriving ball of weird that is the human experience. That you, simply by living your life and your experience, have something to say. The people discussed in this book, the people I spoke to, are all simply ordinary people, sharing their stories. There is a power in your story too, simply because it exists as your story.

This is grace and this is gospel—that our stories have worth because they are ours. That alone makes them worth telling. I hope that you have found some tools within these pages with which to understand and tell your own story. I hope that you find yourself, here, a worthy person just as you are.

Acknowledgments

This book would not have come together without the effort of a whole team of different people and loads of coffee.

To Hannah, the agent who believed in me: thank you for being willing to try something new.

To Adrienne, Chelsea, and the team at Jericho/Hachette: thank you for taking a chance on a first-time angry feminist author. Your shaping of the work has been utterly invaluable to me (and thank you to Wendy Grisham for seeing the potential in the first place).

To Sarah N. Moon, Dani Kelley, Matthew Paul Turner, Rachel Held Evans, Emily Maynard, Tope Charlton, Rachel Coleman, Fr. Shannon Kearns, Alan Hooker, Rod Thomas, Suzannah Paul, and Drs. Greg Dyer, Greg Garrett, and Jenny Bangsund: thanks for believing that I could do this, every step of the way.

To those who volunteered for interviews and took the time to give me thoughtful, gracious answers: this book couldn't exist without you. You know who you are, and you are appreciated.

To the baristas at the Starbucks on Jefferson in downtown Naperville: thanks for keeping me supplied with all those hazelnut soy lattes while I camped out at your tables to write.

ACKNOWLEDGMENTS

To my friends at Coffea in Sioux Falls, who supplied me with more tea than a girl knows what to do with: thanks for keeping me fueled during the editing process.

To my parents, who taught me to read and write before I even got into school: you mean more to me than I could ever express. Thank you.

Notes

1. Kristin Luker, *When Sex Goes to School* (New York: WW Norton and Company, 2006), 53.
2. Stephanie Coontz, *The Way We Never Were* (New York: Basic Books, 1992), 7.
3. Luker, *When Sex Goes to School*, 83.
4. PBS, "Jerry Falwell," *God in America*, http://www.pbs.org/godinamerica/people/jerry-falwell.html.
5. Janice M. Irvine, *Talk About Sex* (UC Press: Berkeley, 2002), 83.
6. Luker, *When Sex Goes to School*, 73.
7. Dave Wright, "A Brief History of Youth Ministry," *The Gospel Coalition* (blog), April 2, 2012, http://thegospelcoalition.org/mobile/article/tgc/a-brief-history-of-youth-ministry.
8. Focus on the Family, "Historical Timeline," http://www.focusonthefamily.com/about_us/news_room/history.aspx.
9. K. Perrin and S. B. DeJoy, "Abstinence-Only Education: How We Got Here and Where We're Going," *Journal of Public Health Policy* 24, no. 3/4 (2003): 446
10. Eric and Leslie Ludy, *When God Writes Your Love Story* (Colorado Springs: Multnomah Books, 2009), 84.
11. Joshua Harris, *I Kissed Dating Goodbye* (Colorado Springs: Multnomah Books, 2003), 94.
12. Rob Bell, *Sex God* (New York: HarperOne, 2007), 132.
13. Matthew 19:3–9.
14. Harris, *I Kissed Dating Goodbye*, 90.
15. John Gill, *Exposition of the Entire Bible* (London: Matthews and Leigh, 1810), http://biblehub.com/commentaries/gill/matthew/5.htm.
16. Ludy and Ludy, *When God Writes Your Love Story*, 111.

17. H. D. M. Spence and Joseph S. Exell, ed, *Pulpit Commentary on the Bible* (Peabody: Hendrickson, 1985), http://biblehub.com/commentaries/pulpit/hebrews/13.htm.

18. Don Hinkle, "Bott Radio blocks Driscoll, replaces segment mid-show," *Baptist Press* (blog), June 17, 2009, http://www.bpnews.net/bpnews.asp?id=30700.

19. Bell, *Sex God*, 53.

20. Mark Regnerus, "The Case For Early Marriage," *Christianity Today* 53 (2009): 8.

21. Kathryn Joyce, "Arrows for the War," *The Nation*, Web, November 9, 2006.

22. Justin Lookadoo and Hayley DiMarco, *Dateable: Are You? Are They?* (Grand Rapids: Hungry Planet, 2005), 77.

23. Tony Reinke, "The Church and the World: Homosexuality, Abortion, and Race with John Piper and Douglas Wilson," *Desiring God*, Web, October 4, 2013.

24. T. F. Charlton, "Conquer, Colonize, and Enslave: On redefining words and rewriting history," *Are Women Human?* (blog), July 22, 2012, http://arewomenhuman.me/2012/07/22/doug-jared-wilson-conquer-colonize-enslave/.

25. Libby Anne, "Christianity, Sin, and Thought Crime," *Love, Joy, Feminism* (blog), November 10, 2011, http://www.patheos.com/blogs/lovejoyfeminism/2011/11/christianity-sin-and-thought-crime.html.

26. Harris, *I Kissed Dating Goodbye*, 87.

27. Dan Amira, "According to Pat Robertson, It's Your Fault Your Husband Cheated On You," *New York Magazine*, Web, May 16, 2012.

28. Joshua Harris, *Sex Is Not the Problem (Lust Is)* (Colorado Springs: Multnomah Books, 2005), 87.

29. Harris, *Sex Is Not the Problem (Lust Is)*, 87.

30. Stanley Hauerwas, *The Hauerwas Reader* (Durham: Duke University Press, 2001), 609.

31. Chimamanda Adichie, "The Danger of a Single Story," *TED Talks* video, 18:49, July 2009, http://www.ted.com/talks/chimamanda_adichie_the_danger_of_a_single_story.

32. Glen Kessler, "Fact Checker: The Claim That 98 Percent of Catholic Women Use Contraception: A Media Foul," *Washington Post*, Web, Feb 17, 2012.

33. Tara Culp-Resser, "Anti-Abortion State Rep Has 'Never Thought About' Why a Woman Would Want an Abortion," *Think Progress*, Web, September 12, 2012.

34. CDC, "HIV Rates among African-Americans (Fact Sheet)," Web, February 6, 2014.

35. Amy Frykholm, "Facts of Life," *The Christian Century* (May 30, 2012): 22.

36. Gorette Amaral, Diana Greene Foster, M Antonia Biggs, Carolyn Bradner Jasik, Signy Judd, and Claire D. Brindis, "Public Savings from the Prevention of Unintended Pregnancy: A Cost Analysis of Family Planning Services in California," *Health Services Research*, Web, October 2007.

37. Abstinence Clearinghouse, *Abstinence 101* (Sioux Falls: Abstinence Clearinghouse, 2007), 2.

38. Ibid., 3–4.

39. John Santelli et al., "Abstinence and Abstinence Only Education: A Review of US Policies and Programs," *The Journal of Adolescent Health* 38 (2005): 72–81.

40. Harris, *I Kissed Dating Goodbye*, 22–23.

41. Sarah Seltzer, "Recent Yale Male Behavior So Sexist the Federal Government Has to Intervene," *Alternet*, Web, April 15, 2011.

42. Kate Harding, "When Sports Culture Meets Rape Culture," *Salon*, Web, July 24, 2009.

43. Abbey Lewis, "Reddit Rape Thread: Why I Don't Care What Rapists Have to Say," *Feminspire*, Web, July 30, 2012.

44. Abstinence Clearinghouse, *Abstinence 101*, 15.

45. Ibid., 18.

46. Cory Copeland, "Sex and the Good Girl," Web, June 21, 2012.

47. Lookadoo and DiMarco, *Dateable*, 35.

48. Ibid., 110.

49. Doug Wilson, "A Tall Tree and a Short Rope," *Blog and Mablog*, Web, Sept 26, 2012.

50. Albert Mohler, "The Bible On Sex: The Way to Happiness and Holiness," albertmohler.com, March 2004.

51. T. F. Charlton, "Evangelical Church Accused of Ignoring Sexual Abuse, 'Pedophilia Ring,'" *Salon*, Web, March 12, 2013.

52. Bobby Ross Jr., "Sovereign Grace Ministries: Courts Shouldn't 'Second-Guess' Pastoral Counseling of Victims," *Christianity Today*, Web, January 25, 2013.

53. Charlton, "Evangelical Church Accused of Ignoring Sexual Abuse, 'Pedophilia Ring,'" *Salon*. Full disclosure: Charlton is a close friend of mine.
54. Dianna Anderson, "Dear Mr. Driscoll," *Jesus Needs New PR/ Matthew Paul Turner.com*, Web, July 8, 2011.
55. C. S. Lewis, *The Lion, The Witch and the Wardrobe* (HarperTrophy: New York, 1950), 86.
56. Andrew Cray, "3 Barriers That Stand Between LGBT Youth and Healthier Futures," *American Progress*, Web, May 29, 2013.